Practical Guide

Earned Value Management

The Most Important Methods and Tools for an Effective Project Control

ROLAND WANNER

Author Contact:
Roland Wanner
E-Mail: info@pm-evm.com
Internet: http://www.pm-evm.com

Distribution:

Amazon Distribution

Disclaimer

This publication is designed to provide competent and reliable information regarding the subject matter covered. However it is not intended as a substitute for legal or other professional services. Readers are urged to consult a variety of sources and professional expert assistance. While every effort has been made to make this book accurate, it may contain typographical and content errors.

The information expressed herein is the opinion of the author, and is not intended to reflect upon any particular person or company. The author and publisher shall have no responsibility or liability with respect to any losses or damage caused, or alleged to be caused, by the information or application of the information contained in this book.

Subjects include: project control, earned value management, project management, project finance, pmbok, pmi, project financial analyst, project controller, Sarbanes-Oxley act, Software, project planning, project performance

Copyright © 2014 by Roland Wanner

All rights reserved. No part of this book may be reproduced, extracted or transmitted by any means, electronic or mechanical, including but not limited to photocopying, recording or by any information storage and retrieval system, without prior written consent of the author.

ISBN: 978-1500850234   Version 1.1 December 2014

Content

Preface 7

1 Project Control Fundamentals — 10
Introduction 10
From Management Accounting to Project Control 12
    Project Control – More Than Just Management Accounting? 12
    Project Control in the PMBOK 13
The Project Control Process 15
    The Project Execution Control Cycle 15
    Internal and External Control 16
    The Project Control Cycle 17

2 The Genesis of Earned Value Management — 19
A new Management Methodology Emerges 19
Current EVM Standards and Guidelines 22

3 Why Do We Need Earned Value Management — 23
What About the Truth? 23
    Sarbanes-Oxley Act - New Legislations Bring New Requirements 23
    We do Not Even Want to Know the Truth! 24
The Baseline/Actual Comparison 26
The Baseline/Actual/Forecast Comparison 27
Who is Going to Tell Me the Future? 30
EVM – Request or Requirement? 31

4 What is Earned Value Management — 34
EVM is More Than Just a Few Key Performance Figures 34
Earned Value Management Definitions 35
Project Management Questions – EVM- Answers 37
Examples of Earned Value Calculations 39
    Example 1: The Farmer "Harvests" Earned Value 39
    Example 2: Software Project 40

5 Project Planning — 42

Project Planning – the Basis for Project Execution 42
    How to Create a Successful Project Schedule 42
    The Planning Process 43
Project Scope Planning 45
    The Work Breakdown Structure 45
    The Work Breakdown Structure and Earned Value Management 49
How to Define Work Packages 50
    The Correct Work Package Size and Duration 51
    The Classification of Work 52
    Work Packages and Earned Value Management 53

6 Control Accounts and Budgeting — 55

Control Accounts 55
Budgeting in Earned Value Management 60
    The Elements of the Contract Baseline 60
    Management Reserve/Contingency Reserve 66
    Schedule Reserve 67
Work Authorization 68

7 Earned Value Management Basis Performance Figures — 71

New EVM-Standard – New EVM Terms 71
PV – Planned Value 71
EV – Earned Value 72
AC – Actual Cost 72
BAC – Budget at Completion 72
Overview of the EVM Performance Figures and Formulas 73

8 The Calculation of the Earned Value — 75

This is the Earned Value 75
EV Methods to Evaluate Work Performance 76
    Percent Start/Percent Finish EV Method 50/50, 25/75, 80/20 78
    50/50 EV Method 78
    0/100 EV Method 79
    Percent Complete EV Method 80

Weighted Milestones EV Method..80
Weighted Milestones with Percent Complete EV Method 82
Units Completed EV Method (Physical Measurement) 82
Apportioned Effort EV Method...84
Level of Effort (LOE) EV Method..84
Implementing EV Methods Correctly..85

9 Project Monitoring with EVM Performance Figures 86
CV – Cost Variance..86
SV – Schedule Variance...86
CPI – Cost Performance Index 87
SPI – Schedule Performance Index 88
Graphical Representation of the CPI and SPI 89
The Behavior of SV, CV, SPI and CPI...90

10 Project Forecasts 92
Forecasts – an Effective Management Tool 92
EAC – Estimate at Completion..94
VAC – Variance at Completion...97
TCPI – To Complete Performance Index 98
ETC – Estimate to Complete..100
Relation Between the EVM-Performance Figures 101
EVM and Risk Management Generate Synergies..............................103

11 Earned Value Management Reporting 105
The Reporting Dilemma..105
Status Reporting With Added Value..106
How to Collect Data in EVM...108
 Data and Variance Analysis 111
The Meaningful Status Report 114
EVM Graphs Bring More Transparency 117
EVM-Reporting in Contracts of the U.S. Government......................118
When Shorter Reporting Cycles Are Meaningful..............................120
Simple EVM On All Your Projects!..123
The Earned Value Management System Criteria..............................125

12 Appendix 131

Earned Value Management Glossar 131
Index 142

Using Earned Value Management, you will receive an extremely powerful project control tool representing problems very early and delivering meaningful predictions about the final project cost and the project end date.

However, Earned Value Management is not a substitute for good project management or a good project manager!

Preface

Too many government and commercial projects fail. Every year more than 60 percent of projects end far over budget or are terminated before project end. This is not new insight: Controlling and reporting of project costs, schedules, technical progress and risks receives an ever increasing importance in project management. Earned Value Management (EVM), now in use for several decades, has provided evidence that it is the most efficient project control methodology. Once the sole domain of the U.S. Department of Defense, EVM has now been in use for a long time also in commercial enterprises around the world. In the early days EVM was criticized due to an inflexible and dogmatic approach. This was overcome in the last 20 years by developments in international standards and adaption to the "real world" and showed, that the basic principles of managing projects with EVM are relatively easy to understand.

This book describes the most important basic principles of Earned Value Management, with its specific performance figures and their effective application in a simple and understandable way. With this very effective tool you bring the necessary transparency and security in the project environment of your company.

Successful project management requires answers to difficult questions, such as:

- The Actual Costs are lower than the planned costs. Does this mean that the project is working well or that it is behind schedule?
- How much does the project cost at project closure and is this still within the budget?
- How efficiently are we using our time and our resources?
- How much will the profit or the ROI be at project closure?

The traditional project cost analysis does not provide answers to these questions. It often deals only with the actual costs of completed work, which are compared with planned costs or the budget. This comparison, however, has a great deficiency – the effective project performance is not considered at all. Earned Value Management, however, is a method for measuring, monitoring and communication of the real performance of a project.

Earned Value Management Answers the Questions

With Earned Value Management, it is possible to calculate statistically the final project costs and the project's completion date long before project closure. Only results count - expenses are costs, but no result. This way, overoptimistic estimates regarding actual project progress will be revealed quickly. EVM performance figures disclose cost and schedule trends very clearly. If these deviate from planned data, it is possible to react early. This is a great strength of EVM, of which project managers and senior management should definitely take advantage. Earned Value Management is a method that can be applied to virtually all types of projects and in any industry.

However, Earned Value Management is:

- not a tool for financial management
- no substitute for good project management/good project leadership
- no security for project success

Earned Value Management is still used little outside large US Government programs and the defense industry. It is one of the least used but most effective cost management tools for projects and programs. There are some reasons for that: the alleged complexity of the surrounding methodology and processes, as well as the effort of gathering the necessary input data, the complex reporting and the integration of the results into other management-information systems. In the past, these reasons were partly a barrier to the spread of EVM. However, in recent years, it was recognized that excessive administration only costs and does not help. Earned Value Management, as it is practiced today, fits into any company that handles various larger projects and programs. EVM is an extraordinarily powerful tool implemented in an appropriate extent.

Earned Value Management reveals a new culture of openness, trust and honesty in the project environment. It provides senior management with full transparency regarding costs, schedules, technical performance and risk data. This improves the relationship between all parties involved in the project.

Are you not afraid of transparency? Do you want to face the truth? Then, you have tackled the right topic with Earned Value Management.

For Whom was This Book Written?

As a buyer of this book, you probably already have some experience in project management. However, in this book you will learn all the additional elements of effective project control with Earned Value Management that will deepen your knowledge.

This book was written primarily for project managers, because project control is a crucial activity of the project manager. Then there are of course project controllers (project financial analysts) who deal daily with this subject. Project portfolio managers will realize when reading this book that they depend on systematic controlling of individual projects so that an effective controlling of the project portfolio can be achieved.

The basis for this book is the standards ANSI/EIA-748, the "Guide to the Project Management Body of Knowledge" (PMBOK® Guide) Fifth Edition 2013 and the "Practice Standard for Earned Value Management" Second Edition 2011 of the PMI. For additional information, documents of the U.S. Department of Defense (DoD) and Department of Energy (DoE) have been used.

This book focuses on individual projects and programs not on controlling of project portfolios.

Project Control Fundamentals

Introduction

Project Control – a Crucial Task of the Project Manager

Project control is the foundation for project success! Does this sound a little arrogant to you? When you have finished reading this book, I am sure you will share my opinion, because the term "project control" is more than just pure number crunching as many believe. Project control is a comprehensive leadership method that extends into personnel management and quality management.

What is project control all about? Roughly speaking, the goal of project control is to systematically monitor the project based on a sound project plan to identify deviations from the planned values as early as possible. The deviations should then be eliminated with effective measures so that the project will return to the planned course. You probably already know this. However, in this book you will read in detail what that includes, how Earned Value Management leverages this process and how it will be implemented in your project.

Project controlling is a key management activity of the project manager, on which he will spend more than 50% of his working time. Do you think this statement is exaggerated and that it cannot be that much? As you will discover in this book, project control is a very broad concept that encompasses many areas of actual project management.

Project Control is More Than Just the Plan/Actual Comparison!

Many project managers, project sponsors and steering committees unfortunately do not know exactly what project control for their project means and what tasks it includes. As an answer to the question of what project control is, project managers would often respond: "Project control? Yes, that's the Baseline/Actual comparison, which I monthly do to check that all work packages are completed as scheduled." Twenty years ago, as a project manager greenhorn, I would have responded the same. Today, I know that the project manager's work comprises mostly project controlling activities and project control significantly contributes to the success of the project. In this book you will learn the methods and techniques employed in project control and how to make your projects even more successful with Earned Value Management.

The Project Controller – the Good Conscience of the Project Manager

For smaller projects, the project manager takes care of project control activities himself. For large projects and programs, he is lucky if he is supported by a project controller or a project financial analyst. This way, the project manager can concentrate on other project management activities and the important stakeholder management activities. The project controller, with his very broad project control and project management knowledge, is a considerable help for the project manager and, therefore, also becomes his "good conscience." If the project manager and project controller are a good team, then an important step toward a successful project is already done.

Project control is management work! The project manager is always responsible for project control – he will, however, gladly delegate a certain part of it to his project controller.

From Management Accounting to Project Control

Like most modern management methods, Management Accounting was first recognized in the United States in the 1920s and a few years later in Europe. Controlling is sometimes interchangeably used with Management Accounting as managerial functions and has to be considered as an independent concept. Controlling could be defined as follows:

Controlling is a forward-looking system of planning, monitoring and control activities for the alignment of corporate events in terms of the achievement of corporate goals and profit goal.

That means: Controlling is a comprehensive control and coordination approach to support senior management and responsible managing bodies at the result-oriented planning and implementation of business activities. If you break down the definitions of controlling to the activities of a controller, as a specialist in corporate planning and control, then you will obtain the following operational tasks:

- Analyzing internal and external factors that affect the profitability and liquidity of the company.
- Participating and consulting at planning and formulation of strategic business objectives. Organizing and coordinating operational sub-planning.
- Monitoring and comparison of actual business development with the short-, medium- and long-term planning. Analysis of variance causes, recommendation of adjustment measures.
- Development and implementation of flexible, transparent methods for analyzing, planning and control.

An important task of the controller is to accompany the management teams in the formulation, agreement and tracking of planned objectives. The controller supports the respective managers for more secure decisions. Below you will find a description of the main tasks of the controller.

Project Control – More Than Just Management Accounting?

The subject of this book is indeed project control. Is project control actually "just" the implementation of "normal" management accounting on projects? This is the opinion of many companies. So unfortunately, their project control is often only a financial control of projects. Project control is more than just a financial control, which focuses on costs (Baseline/Target/-

Actual), budgets, depreciations and some other financial ratios – and this mostly for cost centers or investments.

Applying controlling to projects means to focus on the characteristics of the project: costs, deadlines, project progress, quality, risks, resources, changes, etc. Therefore a project controller is for me more than a "project financial analyst" who only deals with financials.

Project control is an important managerial task in the project and its benefits are still often underestimated. Project control obtains an increasingly important role, not only at the individual project level, but also at the project portfolio level. After all, it is about planning, monitoring and controlling of a larger number of projects in the company.

Project Control in the PMBOK

The comprehensive term "project control," as used in German, is not common in the Anglo-Saxon language. You can also note this quickly if you deal a little further with the PMBOK of the PMI. There you will find only the definitions and descriptions on Planning, Monitoring and Control. This is then also notable in the basic concept of the PMBOK, which consists of "Project Management Processes" and "Project Management Knowledge Areas."

The following ten project control activities of the PMBOK Guide Fifth Edition are summarized in the "Monitoring and Controlling Process Group":

- Monitor and Control Project Work
- Perform Integrated Change Control
- Validate Scope
- Control Scope
- Control Schedule
- Control Costs (incl. Earned Value Management)
- Control Quality
- Control Communications
- Control Risks
- Control Procurements
- Control Stakeholder Engagement

In the following figure you can see how the different Process Groups overlap themselves during the project life cycle. If a project consists of several phases, then you will find these Process Groups within each phase. That means each phase has an Initiating and Planning Process, and in each phase something is created. Monitoring and Controlling will take place during each phase and each phase has a Closing Process.

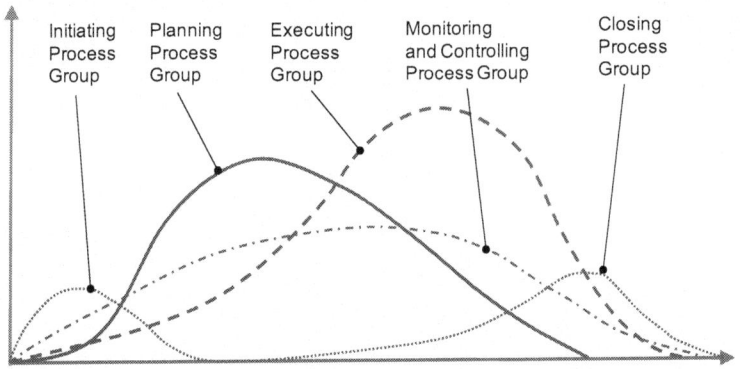

Figure 1: The Interaction between the individual „Process Groups" of the PMBOK

The Project Control Process

In the previous sections, you learned about project control according to PMBOK. At this point, I want to summarize what project control consists of from the process perspective.

Project Planning:

1. Project Implementation Planning
2. Project Scope Planning
3. Activity Sequencing
4. Resource Planning
5. Organization Planning
6. Project Cost Planning
7. Project Scheduling
8. Project Budget Planning

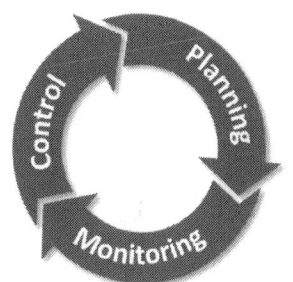

Project Monitoring

1. Compare Plan and Actual data, determine deviations
2. Analyze and document deviations

Project Control:

1. Define and plan responses
2. Decide on responses
3. Delegate responses

The Project Execution Control Cycle

The project execution control cycle gives you a better understanding of the dynamic interaction of the core elements of project management (project planning, project monitoring and project control) and project execution.

The project goals defined by the project sponsor (or client) form the basis for project planning and the creation of the project schedule. During project planning, the project manager deals with the project-related deliverables and tasks. Through "controlling," he passes these, in the form of work packages and coordination measures and instructions, on to the project team. The project team then executes these tasks. The developing results (Deliverables) will be compared during project monitoring activities with

Project Control Fundamentals

the planned values or the given goals (Baseline/Target/Actual comparison). The results of these monitoring activities will then be incorporated back into project planning. This process will continuously repeat itself until project completion.

As you can see in the figure blow, project control is a separate process with the two main elements " Monitoring" and " Control," which are links between project planning and project execution.

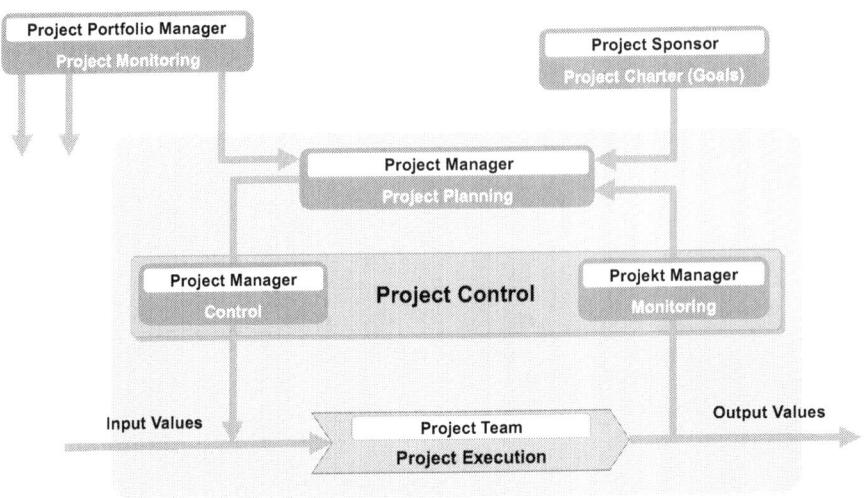

Figure 2: The project control cycle

Internal and External Control

Project control can be divided into internal and external control. The "project internal" control process takes place within the project; the project external control process takes place outside project execution, e.g., through project portfolio management or an external management accountant. Internal project control is used by the project manager to manage accordingly influencing factors or disturbances, changes in project objectives, planning and estimation errors, etc. This with the aim to complete the project successfully and preferably within the defined project scope.

External project control is carried out outside of project execution, usually by project portfolio management. External project control plans and monitors the entire project landscape of the company or of a business unit and reports major project internal issues or cross-project issues and possible control measures to the project portfolio steering committee, which will decide on the appropriate measures.

The Project Control Cycle

One of the most important instruments of the project manager is the internal project control cycle. It is the core of the project execution control cycle that you have learned about, and consists of the main elements: planning, monitoring and control. By no means is this control cycle an invention of project management, but instead describes in general the management process and corresponds to a modern understanding of leadership.

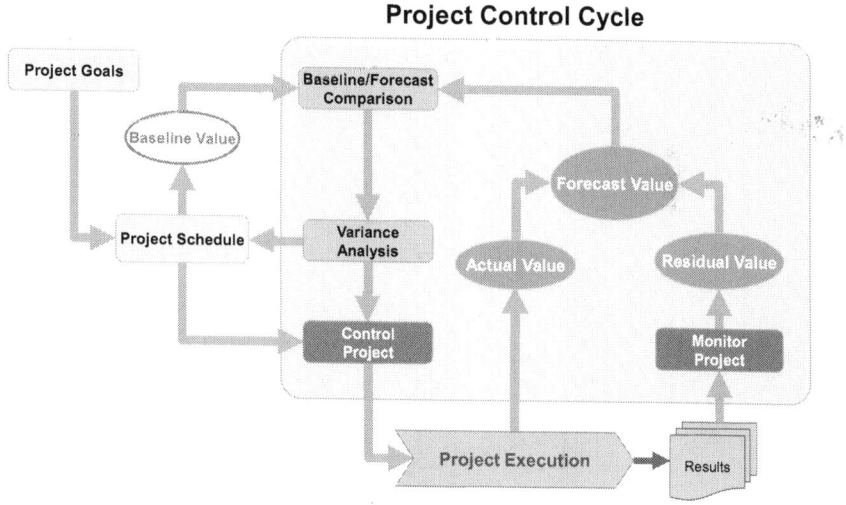

Figure 3: The internal project control cycle

As you can see in Figure 3, the project goals are the basis of project planning and the creation of the project schedule. Based on the project schedule, the project manager (via control project) may pass on the tasks to the project team. Based on the hours worked by the project team and a possible consumption of additional resources, actual values will be reported, e.g., 84 working hours. The achieved results up to that date will be verified and the degree of completion determined. Derived from that, you determine how much work is still to be done (Residual Value) until the result is completed, for example 42 working hours. The Actual Value and the Remaining Value result in the "new" Target Value. The Target Value (126 working hours) will be compared with the Baseline Value (100 working hours). If this comparison results in a greater difference, then a deviation analysis must be performed. This may cause a change of the project schedule and may require a controlling action.

The project internal control process is a relatively simple management theory, which still represents a challenge for all involved. In a project, it will pass through again and again consciously or unconsciously. The frequency in which it will done depends of course, on various factors, such as the complexity, size and duration of the project.

The Genesis of Earned Value Management

A new Management Methodology Emerges

Projects – a Risky Business for the DoD

In commercial companies, success or failure depends mainly on profit and customer satisfaction. On the other hand, the multi-billion expensive programs of the Department of Defense (DoD) are facing a difficult environment. Project problems often led to unpredicted postponements and cost increases or reductions of production units. Programs had to be continued because weapons systems were needed - sometimes at drastically higher cost than estimated at the beginning and at lower production units as desired.

In contrast to commercial projects, military programs are often tasked with developing things that were never done before. The DoD recognized in the early 1950s that the increasingly complex weapons system contracts required more effective management techniques than the ones that were used in the industry at this time. Also, for its own protection, new techniques have been developed since the DoD, to a large extend, assigns the contracts to the private industry.

Under these conditions, Earned Value Management was developed. In the upcoming sections you will learn more about how Earned Value Management has evolved from the factory floor in the late 18th century until today.

Versions of Earned Value Management Have Long been Around

The genesis of modern project management dates back to the major projects of the United States during the Second World War. NASA and the DoD were at that time, and are even today, on the forefront of modern project management and this also applies to Earned Value Management.

The Earned Value method was applied, however, already in the late 18th century by industrial engineers in American factories. For years, these engineers did what most corporate managers currently omit: They used an approach to evaluate the efficiency of performance. The engineers had related actual work performed with its planned values and the actual accumulated costs. Thus, the performance of their production was measured and the result of this approach is the true basis of Earned Value Management.

The U.S. Navy was the Pioneer

In 1917, Henry Gantt developed one of the first modern project management techniques - the bar chart (Gantt chart). In the mid-50s, the U.S. Navy started the Polaris program, which developed submarine-based missiles. Up to this point, there were no suitable project management and controlling techniques for such technologically complex programs. Therefore, in connection with this program, the "Program Evaluation Review Technique" (PERT) was developed within a few weeks. Since PERT was a great success, it was officially implemented in the U.S. Navy as a network planning technique in 1958.

PERT was further developed several times, as PERT/cost and PERT/time, but it did not survive the mid-60s. Presently, the term PERT is still used as a generic term for a network plan. However, the heart of PERT/cost survived as the Earned Value concept.

The DoD Further Developed EVM

In 1967, the PERT/cost concept was a key element in the DoD-Instruction DoDI 7000.2 (Performance Measurement for Selected Acquisitions) for DoD contractors. This stipulated for the contractors the method "Cost/-Schedule Control Systems Criteria" (C/SCSC) for contracts for which the government had some or all of the risks of cost exceeding. In practice, it was called "C-specs." The criteria were first established by the Air Force in the early '60s. The DoD defined 35 criteria that set minimum requirements for a project management system. Despite these instructions, the C/SCSC-criteria were mostly only integrated on paper and were referred to as exaggerated "nitpicking." However, they were not perceived as a true management tool.

Despite the impressive obtained results when using Earned Value Management, the DoD had made initiatives to remove excessive and ineffective components of the C/SCSC in recent years. In 1996, the new 32 Earned

Value Management System Criteria (EVMS) were completed in a simpler, more comprehensive form.

One of the DoD's primary objectives with the introduction of Earned Value Criteria was that all project participants worked with the same management control system. This enabled the DoD to implement accurate project monitoring throughout the project life cycle. Earned Value Management provides senior management at each stage with an effective tool and a common language.

Important EVM Milestones:

- 1958 PERT and PERT/Cost (Milestone Charts and Rate-of Expenditure Curves, Dollars Spent vs Estimates of Percent)
- 1963 Earned Value Concept (MINUTEMAN)
- 1964 Cost Accomplishment Concept (TITAN III)
- 1966 Air Force Cost/Schedule Planning and Control Specification (C/SPCS)
- 1967 DOD—35 Cost/Schedule Control Systems Criteria (C/SCSC) (DODI 7000.2) "C-Specs"
- 1972 DOD—Revised DODI 7000.2 and Issued the Joint Implementation Guide (JIG)
- 1991 DODI 5000.2 replaces DODI 7000.2
- 1996 DODR 5000.2-R replaces DODI 5000.2, C/SCSC revised from 35 to 32 criteria
- 1996 Revised JIG—Renamed Earned Value Management Implementation Guide (EVMIG)
- 1998 ANSI/EIA-748, "Earned Value Management Systems" (EVMS) took over the 32 Criteria DODI 5000.2

Current EVM Standards and Guidelines

In a relatively long development time for a modern management method, various standards and guidelines have been created. The following list contains the most important and, at present, current documents. However, it is not complete:

- American National Standards Institute (ANSI)/Electronic Industries Alliance (EIA) ANSI/EIA-748-C 2014"Earned Value Management Systems"
- NDIA PMSC ANSI/IEA-748-B Standard for Earned Value Management Systems Intent Guide, August 2012, PDF
- Canadian General Standards Board Project Performance Management CAN/CGSB-187.2-99
- Earned Value Management Committee, Council of Standards Australia (2003). AS4817-2006: Project Performance Measurement Using Earned Value. Sydney, Australia: Standards Australia International, LTD.
- Earned Value Management APM Guideline for the U.K. Buckinghamshire, United Kingdom: The Association for Project Management 2002.
- DoD Earned Value Management Implementation Guide (EVMIG) Principles - Industry-developed set of 32 standards adopted for use by DoD in 1996 for evaluation of contractor management systems. October 2006
- DOD's C-SSR Joint Guide: Cost-Schedule Management of Non-Major Contracts

PMI Standards

- Project Management Body of Knowledge (PMBOK® Guide), Fifth Edition 2013 (Chapter 7.4.2.1)
- Practice Standard for Earned Value Management, PMI Global Standard 2011

Why Do We Need Earned Value Management

What About the Truth?

Sarbanes-Oxley Act - New Legislations Bring New Requirements

In the years 2000-2003 there was, without question, a series of spectacular corporate failures, primarily in the energy and telecommunications sectors: Enron, WorldCom, Global Crossing and Parmalat in Europe - just to mention the best known. These financial scandals cost investors much money and were, among other things, triggered by questionable accounting methods, poor management or lack of internal controls. Some senior managers were cast in a very bad light because of this scandal and the confessed in lengthy court processes as a result.

Is poor project management a crime? The answer may be "Yes," according to the Sarbanes-Oxley Act. After the various financial scandals became public, at end of July 2002 the U.S. Congress passed the Sarbanes-Oxley Act (SOX). The spotlight is now one every CFO and CEO to give an accurate portrayal of the company's true financial condition. The Sarbanes-Oxley Act requires the CFO and CEO, on pain of heavy penalties, to confirm the truth and completeness of the published annual report. The audit firm is required to comment on whether the report of management on the quality of controls applies.

The Sarbanes-Oxley Act is mandatory for all American companies and government organizations, as well as for all foreign companies listed on U.S. stock exchanges. Central point of the Sarbanes-Oxley Act is the independence of the internal audit functions, but most important are the new, strict corporate governance rules.

The True Status of the Projects Counts

The new rules oblige senior managers, among others, to reveal the true state of their large, multi-year projects. When cost overruns are not foreseen for projects, and therefore not clearly presented in the financial report, this has a significant impact on the income of future periods.

The Sarbanes-Oxley Act requires companies to disclose what processes create the financial statements and how reliable they are implemented. Needless to say, projects have a significant influence on many companies' financial statements.

What could help project-oriented companies comply with Sarbanes-Oxley Act? If your project management processes are not yet clearly defined, then you have in accordance with section 404 of the Sarbanes-Oxley Act, to catch up with some work. This obligation can be fulfilled only with proven project management methods and in particular with Earned Value Management. With Earned Value Management you use best practice in project planning and project control. You have an excellent tool to meet the required internal processes and control instruments in accordance with Section 404 of SOX.

EVM supports compliance with SOX as follows:

- proven and documented project management processes
- no subjective estimates, but objective numbers that correspond to the principle of prudence
- financial predictions that the senior management can trust, because they are calculated with recognized EVM formulas and performance figures.

The legal liability for poor project management and improper financial predictions lies not only on the shoulders of the CEO or the CFO. Senior management and the project manager also have the legal liability when it comes to financial mismanagement of projects.

We do Not Even Want to Know the Truth!

The financial scandals that have become known in recent years were only the tips of the iceberg that looked out of the water. Some levels below, where the iceberg is wider, much more money is at stake. In virtually every company, large-scale projects are carried out, some of which take several years. In many companies, one is often not aware of, how much money is at stake because these projects lacks many professionals from project portfolio management and project control.

These specialists work with proven methods and meaningful indicators and thus bring transparency to the project environment. This transparency is required by newer laws with the aim to uncover maladministration and financial problems in projects at an early stage. Up to now, there have been attempts in many companies to cover up the facts. In other words, they didn't want to face the truth. The new laws, however, bring a more open information culture in companies - which not everyone wants.

SOX to hell! Again, no bonus at year-end.

The Baseline/Actual Comparison

What is the status of the project? You get different answers to this question, depending on whom you ask. At steering committee presentations the following charts are often presented to the senior management:

- Baseline/Actual Cost comparison
- Gantt chart with or without progress bars

Is it possible to read the true state of the project from these charts? Hardly. But it apparently seems that the senior management is always satisfied. One of the senior managers may still ask for obvious missed deadlines if the schedule delay will be able to catch up, but that is all.

Traditional cost analysis is concerned with the Actual Cost of work performed, which is compared with the planned costs at reporting date. The Baseline/Actual comparison is the simplest form of project monitoring. In this, the deviation of the actual values (e.g., Actual Costs, actual working hours, actual amount of work) is determined by the corresponding Plan values on the reporting date.

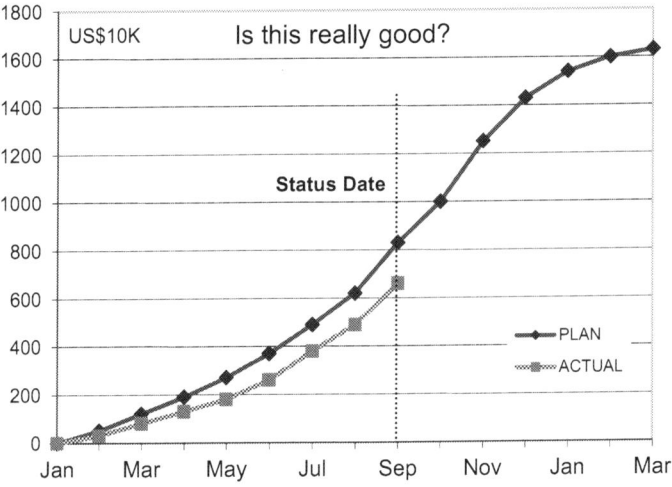

Figure 4: Line graph of baseline/actual comparison

Watch the Baseline/Actual comparison in Figure 4 and Figure 5 for the reporting date 1 September. Should this project manager be satisfied or rather concerned? It seems that the current costs are a lot lower than the planned cost. That is obviously good news!

Why Do We Need Earned Value Management

The additional Gantt chart provides some more information because the black progress bars are drawn – which is not often seen. You can see a delay on the schedule, "which can be safely caught up again." With the combination of his two diagrams you can draw a clearer statement. Nevertheless, as long as you do not look at the planned cost of work performed, you really do not know, if good or bad news must be reported. This is merely one of the pieces of missing information that, for example, Earned Value Management provides.

The statement of the Baseline/Actual comparison is practically worthless because it gives no clear statement about the status of the project. This requires both: cost and time information, together with the degree of work completed must be considered. To obtain a reasonably useful statement, the Baseline/Actual comparison needs to be supplemented at least by a Gantt chart with progress bars or through a milestone trend analysis. Project evaluations regarding content give additional clarity.

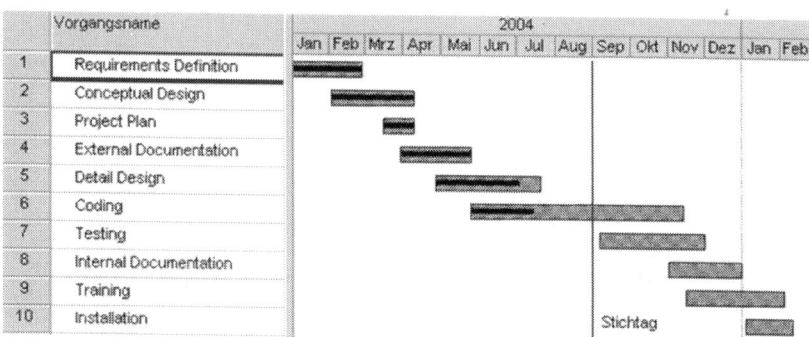

Figure 5: Gantt Chart with black progress bars

The Baseline/Actual/Forecast Comparison

You have certainly heard of the Forecast/Actual comparison. In the project environment, many people talk about the Forecast/Actual comparison when they probably mean the Baseline/Actual comparison.

A project baseline is defined when the original plan (original scope, cost and schedule) of the project is frozen, whereas the project schedule is a living document. The baseline is used to measure how performance deviates from the plan. The project's baseline must be completely defined and documented before project execution and control activities can begin.

Is Forecast the same as Baseline? In a business sense, one speaks of Forecast Cost when it comes to the costs that should be incurred at the achieved level of performance according to plan. In engineering, the Forecast Value is a predetermined value, which should be achieved by a dynamic value – the actual value. Now what exactly is the meaning of Forecast Value in the project environment?

In project control, one tries to go one step further with the Baseline/Actual/Forecast comparison than with the usual Baseline/Actual comparison. Here, project progress is measured and analyzed not only qualitatively but also quantitatively. The analysis of the differences and the calculation of the Residual Values then provide the basis for predicting the final cost of the project.

Figure 6 shows what exactly is meant by the Baseline/Actual/Forecast comparison. Here, the Baseline/Actual/Forecast values have the following meanings:

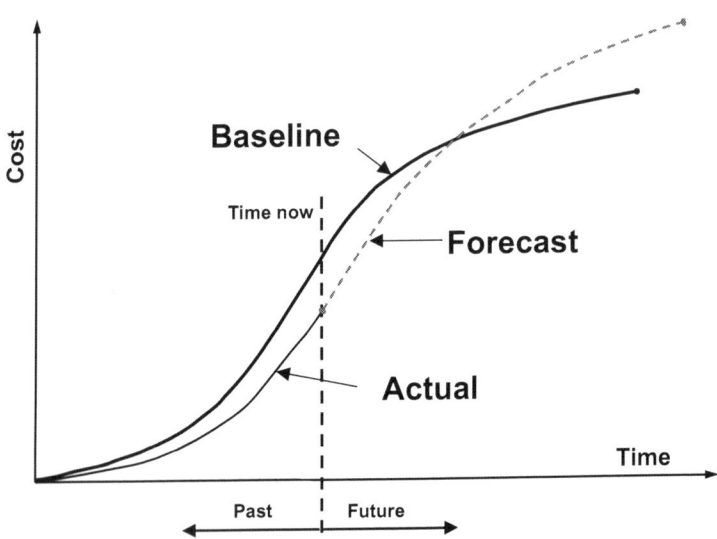

Figure 6: The Baseline//Forecast/Actual comparison of projects

The **Baseline Values** (Planned Values) correspond to the values of the frozen base planning. They apply to the whole project duration; this implies left and right of the reporting date (time now). The Baseline Values are only changed at an "exceptional case", e.g., if the project scope changes.

The **Actual Values** correspond to the Actual Costs, which were entered in the accounting system. The Actual Values can only be obtained for the past. Therefore, they are left of "Time now."

The **Remaining Values** are not shown in Figure 6. They correspond to the Remaining Cost of the still unfinished work, until the work package or project is finished. The Remaining Costs are estimated by the project manager or the work package manager according to the remaining work.

The **Forecast Values** (Scheduled Values) correspond to the sum of the Actual Costs and the Residual Values. The Forecast Values are predictions. Therefore, they are right of "Time now," meaning in the future. They define the "current planning."

From this description you will see that on the left of "Time now" only the comparison of the Baseline and Actual Values is possible. In the future, which is on the right side of "Time now," only Baseline and Forecast Values can be compared with each other. Only on "Time now," can Baseline, Actual and Forecast Values be compared. This corresponds to the "real" Baseline/Actual/Forecast comparison in the commercial sense. Following, you will find a simple example of a Baseline/Actual/Forecast calculation.

Phase	Planned Value	Actual Value	Remaining Value	Forecast Value
Conceptual Design	200	220	0	220
Program Specification	300	330	0	330
Coding	600	400	220	620
Documentation	100	20	70	90
User Manual Production	400	0	400	400
Debugging	500	0	500	500
Sum	2100	970	1190	2160

Figure 7: Example of a Baseline/Actual/Forecast calculation at a software project

At this point, you might ask: "What else do we need? This way, we know exactly the actual status of the project and what is still ahead of us." I admit: Using the Baseline/Actual/Forecast comparison, you can obviously make better predictions, as you determine the Residual Values and obtain the Forecast costs. But even the Baseline/Actual/Forecast comparison does not provide you with enough reliable data. What you lack is the current physical completed work, i.e., the physical degree of completion and the resulting calculated completion value, which corresponds to the Earned Value.

The Residual Values are mostly based on subjective estimates and are often too optimistic, in other words too low. To obtain better conclusions about the project status and to get more reliable predictions, you can use the Earned Value and the performance figures of Earned Value Management.

Who is Going to Tell Me the Future?

The future of most companies depends heavily on projects, because one who wants to sell new products or a new service, must develop first. But what about the health of your projects? Do you have meaningful information at an early stage, when the project will end and at what costs? Will senior management be flooded with informative charts, trends and forecasts? Does each executive board member know the facts about the most important projects, and where an urgent need for necessary action is? The answer in most companies is the same: No! There is no transparency.

Although the future of many companies depends heavily on projects, it is not understandable why there is so little attention paid to this. If an important project fails, it could mean the death knell for a company. It is therefore crucial to have tools available that provide clear statements about time, cost, and project progress. Using Earned Value Management, all project participants receive a tool that creates such a transparency about the state of the projects, which until now was unattainable. There is currently no other technique that integrates project scope, cost and schedule to such a high extent.

How Long Does it Take?

Do you address the future of your project from time to time? Then it's desirable for you to obtain answers to the following questions:

- How much work still needs to be done?
- How much time is still necessary?
- When is the actual project completion date?
- How much money will the project need until it is completed?

If you remember these questions on family road trips, when the kids always asked: "Are we there yet? How long does it take?" then the above questions are not exceptional. As a passenger on a trip wonders, how long it will take until arriving at the destination, so do managers need to know how long a project will take, and how much it will cost. They should be concerned about the future of their projects.

The future holds many dangers – and no one can predict them. With Earned Value Management you at least have a tool, with which it is possible to statistically calculate the project end cost and end date long before the planned completion time. The past serves as a basis, providing data to determine corrections for the future. Course corrections are easier when you have time to make small adjustments in the project; however, it is too late when you already have an iceberg in front of you. An ideal, complementary tool to EVM is risk management, which addresses future uncertainty. With this combination, you have your project uncertainties much better under control!

Learn more about project forecasts in Chapter 10.

Figure 8: Too late to initiate course corrections

EVM – Request or Requirement?

In many companies, complex and often very expensive projects are carried out, which means economic risks should not to be underestimated. Therefore, a great need exists for consistent project status information, which also makes predictions about the project's end date or the final cost of the project, among other items. A large part of this need is fulfilled only by Earned Value Management.

Many companies, including also in the European Union, are forced to apply Earned Value Management. Any company who accepts projects or orders from the U.S. Department of Defense, the U.S. Government or its subcontractors will automatically be faced with Earned Value Management for large projects[1], which is required. I can well imagine that even the European Union or European Government or Authority will issue a similar regulation in the near future.

Below you will find some typical examples of American regulations and standards that need to comply with EVM, or whose fulfillment is supported through EVM:

- Government Performance and Results Act of 1993 (GPRA)
- FASA, Title V; 1994
- Clinger-Cohen Act; 1996,
- Office of Management and Budget (OMB), Circular A-11, Part 7
- Sarbanes-Oxley Act, 2002
- DoD Instruction 5000.2, "Operation of the Defense Acquisition System," May 12, 2003

The Sarbanes-Oxley Act, passed by the U.S. Congress at the end of July 2002, has caused more companies to take a more accurate look at their projects. The spotlight is now one every CFO and CEO to give an accurate portrayal of their true financial condition. The new, strict Corporate Governance rules and strengthened internal audit require new tools to ensure more transparency. Earned Value Management is one of them.

---

[1] see also Page 116 „EVM-Reporting in Contracts of the U.S. Government

My Project is too Small for EVM

For small projects, the aim is to keep the "administrative burden" as low as possible. That is why one often omits proven project management methods, since these are supposedly only a burden. However, one underestimates the fact that a bunch of small projects also cost a lot of money. Why should you then waive on an appropriate project control?

The standard ANSI/EIA-748 writes something like: The rules and processes of the applying companies determine the extent and project size in which EVM is used. According to the Australian EVM-standard AS4817 – "EVM is applicable to all types and sizes of projects in any industry."

From my experience, Earned Value Management can be used reasonably from a project size of about 700,000 Dollars.

What is Earned Value Management

EVM is More Than Just a Few Key Performance Figures

In this chapter you will learn what the most important figure of EVM, the "Earned Value," means. You will see in more detail what Earned Value Management is and what kind of questions Earned Value Management can answer during project execution.

Earned value management is more than just a few numbers. It is a structured project management methodology with four main goals:

1. Defines the performance measurement baseline
2. Measures, analyzes, and represents the performance of a project
3. Shows schedule and budget deviations during project execution
4. Predicts the estimated time of project completion and the final project cost

To perform these four main tasks, Earned Value management provides consistent, numerical performance figures to assess and compare projects and to create predictions.

The fundamental principles of Earned Value Management are:

- All project work is planned until project closure – earlier work more precise and later work in less detail.
- The work is decomposed in work packages, which are given to a responsible group of people or an organization.

- Project scope, schedule and cost estimates are integrated into a baseline that can be used to measure project progress.
- All Actual costs are registered.
- Deviations from the defined baseline are analyzed, impacts predicted and the final project result estimated based on current project progress.
- Changes on the baseline are controlled.
- Earned value management information is incorporated in the management process of the organization.

Earned Value Management Definitions

The terminology surrounding Earned Value Management can often be confusing. It is frequently assumed that Earned Value Analysis and Earned Value Management are the same, which is wrong. "Analysis" only describes a small fragment of this management methodology. Others speak of Earned Value Management, but attempt to describe the Earned Value with some other performance indicators, like CPI and SPI. This is not completely correct as well, since Earned Value Management incorporates more.

The three different definitions of Earned Value used in this book all have their own meaning. This figure describes the hierarchy of the different terms.

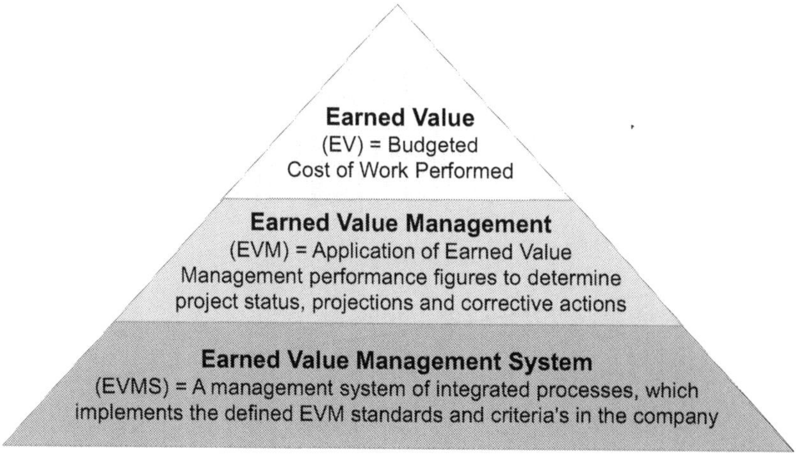

Earned Value
(EV) = Budgeted Cost of Work Performed

Earned Value Management
(EVM) = Application of Earned Value Management performance figures to determine project status, projections and corrective actions

Earned Value Management System
(EVMS) = A management system of integrated processes, which implements the defined EVM standards and criteria's in the company

Figure 9: Hierarchy of EVM Terms

Earned Value Management System (EVMS)

An Earned Value Management System is a number of integrated processes, which implements the defined standards and criteria. The standard ANSI/EIA-748 (Earned Value Management Systems) defines the appropriate guidelines. In its simplest form, EVMS can be implemented without software, which is merely a means to an end and increases productivity, allows for a more economical implementation of EVM and enhances the management of complex projects. EVMS is not software.

Earned Value Management (EVM)

Earned Value Management is a program management tool, which integrates project scope, schedule and cost parameters. This allows comprehensive project monitoring with various performance indicators as well as forecasts about the final project costs and the project end date.

Earned Value (EV)

The Earned Value is the budgeted cost of work performed. If the EV is compared with the planned work and the Actual Costs, performance and progress of the project can be determined.

Project Management Questions – EVM- Answers

Earned Value Management answers the following project management standard question in an ongoing project:

Project Management Questions	EVM Performance Measures
How are we doing cost-wise?	**Cost Analysis & Forecasting**
- Are we under or over our budget?	- Cost Variance (CV)
- How efficiently are we using our resources?	- Cost Performance Index (CPI)
- How efficiently must we use our remaining resources?	- To Complete Performance Index (TCPI)
- What is the project likely to cost?	- Estimate at Completion (EAC)
- Will we be under or over budget?	- Variance at Completion (VAC)
- What will the remaining work cost?	- Estimate to Complete (ETC)
How are we doing time-wise?	**Schedule Analysis & Forecasting**
- Are we ahead of or behind schedule?	- Schedule Variance (SV)
- How efficiently are we using our time?	- Schedule Performance Index (SPI)
- When is the project likely to be completed?	- Estimate at Completion (Time) (EACt)

Figure 10: Project Management Questions – Earned Value Management Answers

If EVM reveals the project manager, that the project is behind schedule or over budget, he can use the EVM methodology to help identify:

- Where problems are occurring
- Whether the problems are critical or not
- What it will take to get the project back on track

You will learn more details about the Earned Value Management Performance Indicators listed above starting on page 71.

The Earned Value is not found in the previous table. Why? The Earned Value is "only" a tool to calculate the EVM performance metrics. However, it is the key element, because you cannot calculate the performance metrics without the Earned Value.

The Earned Value Determines Physical Progress

I will show you briefly what the Earned Value means, which will help you to better understand the two simple examples on the following pages.

With the help of the Earned Value, you determine the value creation, respectively the "true project performance" at the status date. The Earned Value is easiest to equate with the physical progress of the project. As the term correctly describes, something was achieved (earned) through the input of a certain effort.

The Earned Value is the value of the work performed at a defined time, based on the planned (budgeted) value for this work.

Earned value used to be called *"Budgeted Cost of Work Performed (BCWP)."* This term describes the Earned Value perfectly. The Earned Value creates a quantitative basis for the calculation of time and cost deviations during project execution. Earned Value Management also makes it possible to estimate the project completion date and final project costs far ahead of time. This makes it possible to discover plan deviations early and to react quickly with appropriate actions.

Examples of Earned Value Calculations

You may wonder: "What is so special about the Earned Value? It is only a performance figure that measures something." To satisfy your curiosity a little, here you will find two simple examples that explain the basic idea of the Earned Value. Starting on page 76, you will find out in more detail how these calculations work.

Example 1: The Farmer "Harvests" Earned Value

Today, the weather is fine. This is why farmer Paul thought about doing a lot. His meadow comprises 150 acres and he plans to harvest 90 acres today. He starts early in the morning, but he is interrupted several times during his work. There is a small emergency in the stable, he has to help out a neighboring farmer for a short time and his mowing machine has a small defect, but he can fix it quickly being a good technician. For lunch on the meadow, he has only a very short time left. In the evening, the farmer returns tired from the big meadow. Unfortunately, he has not achieved everything that he had planned. In Figure 11, you see the balance of the day and in the following table you can find the corresponding calculation.

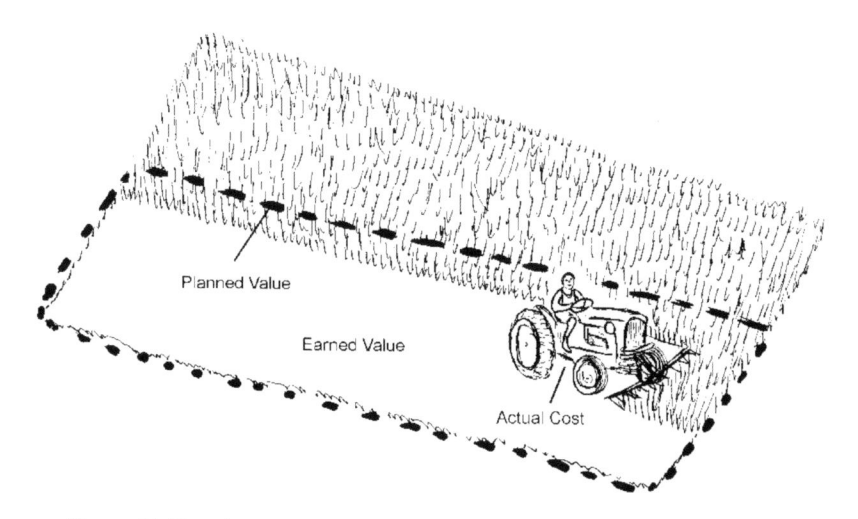

Figure 11: Visual presentation of the Earned Value

Work/Effort	Value	Sum
Planned Work: (Planned Value) 90 acres harvested meadow	$450	$450
Effective Work Performance: (Earned Value) 75 acres harvested meadow	$375	$375
Effort for this Work Performance: (Actual Cost)	Tractor Cost $150 Diesel $30 Labor Cost $200 Food $10	$390

Figure 12: Example: Harvest meadow Earned Value calculation

The results show that Paul has not achieved what he planned on this day. That means that he was not as efficient as planned. Moreover, the effort for the work accomplished was a little higher than expected. What all this means and what consequences there are for the farmer, you will see later when we discuss the EVM performance figures in detail. The goal of Example 1 was to identify what Earned Value figuratively means, namely that something is harvested.

Example 2: Software Project

As a project manager of a software development project, you must determine the project status at end of month. You also want to know what percentage of the project has been completed and whether it will be completed on time. At first glance, this is not so obvious. In the bar chart on the next page, you can only see the planned and actual duration of the activities.

As you already know, the Earned Value is the value of the completed work at a certain time, based on the planned (budgeted) value for this work. Since the Conceptual Design and the Program Specification are finished, we now have earned a value of 500 planned hours. We have decided to provide the activities that are started only recently, 25% of Earned Value and in further steps 50%, 75% and 100%. So we can waive on subjective estimates, like 37%. The activity Coding is in progress and receives 25% Earned Value of the Planned Value (150) and Documentation has also been started recently and receives 25% Earned Value (25) of its Planned Value. In total, we have earned 675 hours. What percentage of the project is now completed? Using Earned Value Management, we calculate a value of 35%

completion, i.e. 675 spent budgeted hours divided by 1900 total budgeted hours.

When we now look at the chart below, we are slightly behind schedule. This can be deceiving because the duration is shown, but not the work. What we lack in this example is the Planned Value to the status date for each activity. Then, we could make a clear statement about the status of each activity. The spent hours (Actual Cost) show the effort that we have needed to compile the Earned Value. In conclusion, one can say that the project is probably slightly behind schedule and will likely cost more at project closure than planned. This example perhaps overextends you a little. No problem! In the next chapters, we will deal with all the details of this example in depth.

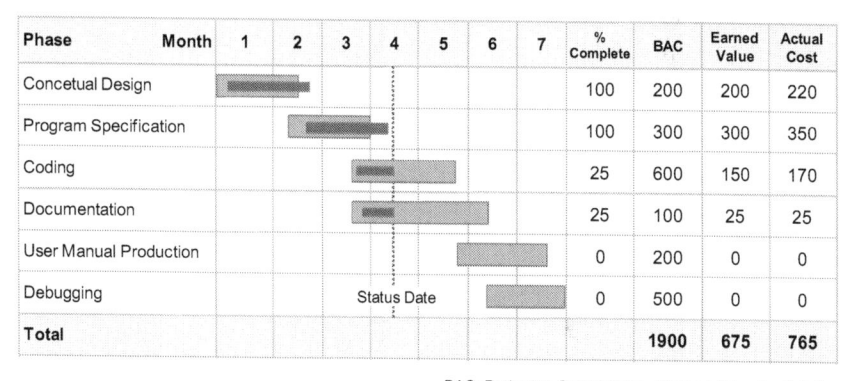

Phase	Month	1	2	3	4	5	6	7	% Complete	BAC	Earned Value	Actual Cost
Concetual Design									100	200	200	220
Program Specification									100	300	300	350
Coding									25	600	150	170
Documentation									25	100	25	25
User Manual Production									0	200	0	0
Debugging					Status Date				0	500	0	0
Total										1900	675	765

BAC=Budget at Completion = Planned Value for Activity

Figure 13: Example of a simple Earned Value calculation for a software project

Project Planning

Project Planning – the Basis for Project Execution

Project planning is one of the most important techniques of project management. It is so important that many believe that project planning is "project management". This is of course a very narrow perspective - and yet not entirely wrong: Without profound planning, a project will never be a success!

I consider project planning, without a doubt, instrumental to the project controlling activities. Some of you might disagree. But my answer is: How are you going to monitor and control your project if you do not have a prudent project schedule that makes this even possible? Therefore, in my point of view, it is important that a project controller be familiar with project planning and that a professional schedule be created, which he then can use as the basis for effective monitoring.

How to Create a Successful Project Schedule

The project-specific requirements and goals are the basis of any binding planning. By using the planning steps described in the following chapters, these requirements convert into clear guidelines for project implementation. With these specifications, unfortunately, many project managers quickly plunge on a scheduling tool such as MS Project and begin to structure the project in a brainstorming way to obtain quickly a beautiful bar chart. However, this unstructured planning approach will very soon get its revenge. Only through a systematic structured planning approach will you later execute, monitor and control your project successfully.

Project Planning

The Planning Process

Planning is of crucial importance for a project, because in a project, something is created that was never done before. Therefore, project planning is the mental anticipation of the possible future realities.

"Begin with the end in mind" (Stephen R. Covey)

According to Stephen R. Covey, all things are created twice. There is a mental (first) creation, and a physical (second) creation. The physical creation follows the mental, just as a building follows a blueprint.

The basis of any binding project planning are clearly defined SMART project goals (**S**pecific, **M**easurable, **A**chievable, **R**ealistic, **T**ime-bound) as well as clear requirements and specifications. Defining project goals is not easy, but critical to project success. Therefore, you should spend sufficient time on it, until concrete goals are defined that will be supported by the key stakeholders.

Project planning does not only include a bar chart (Gantt chart) as is often believed. This view is too narrow. According to the PMBOK®, project planning consists of various plans, which are, for small projects, mostly integrated into the "project management plan." The bar chart (schedule) with deadlines, costs and resources is just one of them.

The project management plan describes how the project is executed, monitored and controlled. It integrates and consolidates all sub-plans and baselines of the planning process:

- Plan Scope Management, Scope Baseline
- Plan Schedule Management, Schedule Baseline
- Cost Management Plan, Cost Baseline

In order to execute the project successfully, you have to plan other important activities, which are not, or not directly, related to the bar chart. In addition to project scope cost and schedule the PMBOK® mentions, among others, the following accompanying planning processes:

- Plan Quality Management
- Plan Human Resource Management
- Plan Communication Management
- Plan Risk Management
- Plan Procurement Management
- Plan Stakeholder Management

Project Planning

The detailing of the project plan should be adjusted to the project scope, the complexity, project duration and the information needs of the project. Plan just as much that you can manage the project safely. That means, for a project with a size of 300,000 Dollar and 5 months duration, there will probably be no work breakdown structure with 200 work packages and a 20-page risk management plan.

Figure 14 shows the most important steps of project planning in Earned Value Management that lead to the project baseline. The steps are the same as in normal project planning. Setting clear boundaries for project scope and the work breakdown structure are critical for project success. Additionally, budgets and reserves are planned in more detail than usual.

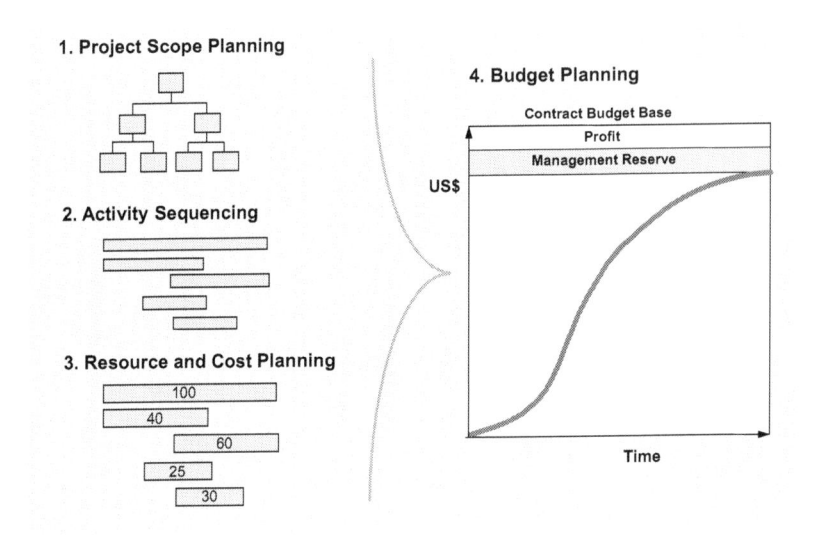

Figure 14: The project planning process in Earned Value Management

In this book, I put the emphasis of project planning on point 1: Project scope planning. This point is the crucial basis for the application of EVM. We will also focus on budgeting more in detail, because EVM has some peculiarities here.

Project Scope Planning

Project scope planning is part of project scope management. Unfortunately this topic is for many project managers still an unknown word. Therefore, later in the project, they are often faced with many project changes and unrestrained project growth. Project scope management deals with planning, monitoring and controlling of project scope. In this section, we focus on project scope planning. A core element of project scope planning is the Work Breakdown Structure (WBS). All projects, not only large and complex ones, require a detailed description of the project work as well as the products and/or services that the project has to deliver.

Defining the WBS – a Crucial Basis for EVM

Once the requirement specification is created, an important first step is done. Of crucial importance for the application of Earned Value Management is the subsequent planning of the Work Breakdown Structure which decomposes project scope in sub-projects, work packages and planning packages. The work breakdown structure is the most valuable, easiest and most underrated project management tool. It is an indispensable basis for the use of Earned Value Management. Therefore, on the following pages you will get to know in detail the Work Breakdown Structure and the definition of work packages. Even if you already know these planning activities – a repetition will certainly provide you with new insights. However, the other project planning activities are just as important and must therefore not be neglected.

The Work Breakdown Structure

Complex Will Instantly Become Easier

In a simple task or a small order, it is usually immediately clear what to do. A project is more complex and requires the decomposing of the work into single manageable units that one can plan and control. The project work must be structured so that it becomes obvious, thus it can be performed effectively and precisely. The result of the decomposition is the Work Breakdown Structure (WBS) as a complete, hierarchical illustration of all elements of a project. This is done classically in the form of an organizational chart, or alternatively as a list illustration with numbering and indentations. However, the list illustration does not have the same informative value as the graphical illustration.

"Divide and conquer!" (Alexander the Great)

Project Planning

The execution of major projects requires a high degree of transparency. Here, the WBS is an important information and controlling tool. The increased planning effort that lies within the careful preparation of the WBS is a worthwhile investment for the definition of work packages. Also, the WBS is indispensable for the creation of the activity sequencing and cost planning, as well as thereon relying project monitoring.

The WBS is also a good tool to get to a common understanding of the project scope. Often, one finds that it is not always so clear what is part of the project and what is not. The WBS is for the project manager what the organizational chart is for the company directors. It shows the full hierarchical arrangement of all elements of a project.

The WBS-structure must also clearly show what elements/products are created by oneself and what come from suppliers (make or buy). The purchase of project elements always means a greater dependence and a greater risk in project execution. Therefore, the "make or buy" decisions should be visible and especially monitored in the WBS.

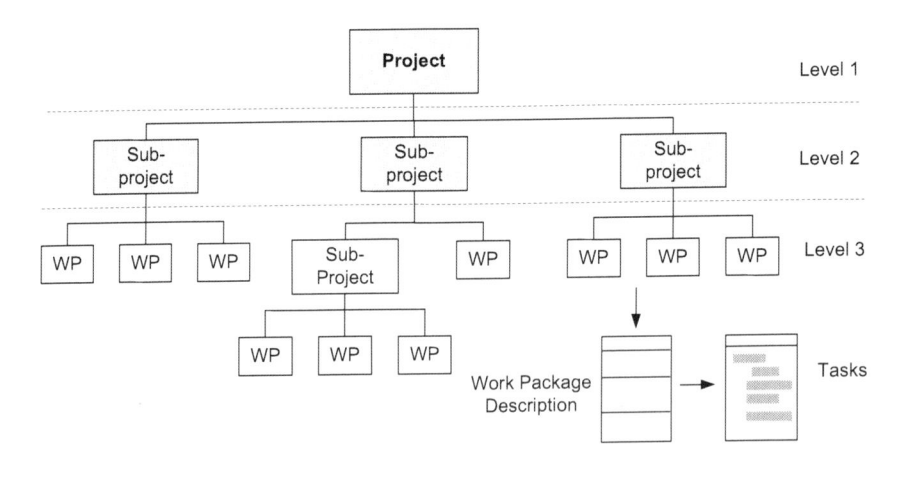

Figure 15: WBS-Definition and Illustration according to DIN 69901

Ways of Project Structuring

"A good work breakdown structure is halfway to reaching the goal." The structuring of a project by tasks or deliverables is important because they are performed by different specialists, teams or companies.

The deliverable-oriented (construction-oriented, product-oriented) WBS decomposes the project into individual items that need to be created/-delivered. This is useful if the project is largely identical with the developed object, for example in building construction, plant construction, or software development.

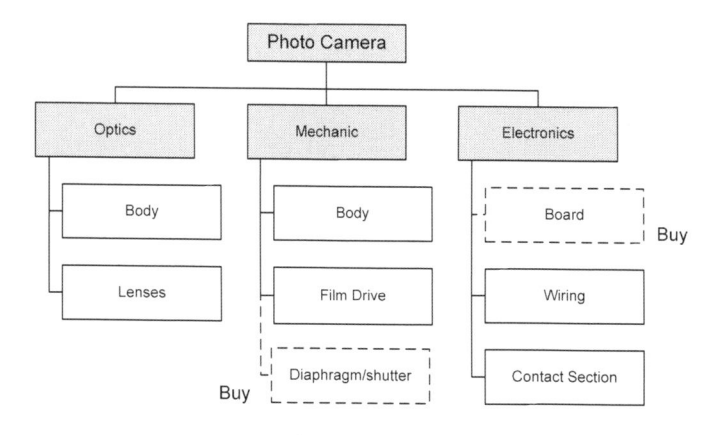

Figure 16: The deliverable-orientated WBS

The task-oriented WBS decomposes the project into individual chores that must be executed. This WBS structure is useful if the project has aspects that are substantially beyond the material object, such as the opening of procurement markets, market introduction of products or collaborations.

The phase-oriented WBS shows on the top level a project phase structure. However, the phase-orientation of the work breakdown structure should not be a dominant design principle, because it will approach too much of the bar chart and does not offer an independent added value.

The mixed-oriented WBS combines the deliverable-orientated and phase-oriented structuring principle. It tries to meet the practice and provides possibilities for different aspects of projects. At the top level, often there are the project phases and on the other levels the functions or tasks.

Project Planning

Defining the Way of Structure

Often, there are disagreements as to whether a WBS should be structured deliverable-oriented, task-oriented or mixed-oriented. Therefore, many companies stipulate the structure or have standard work breakdown structures for similar types of projects. Whenever possible, you should build up the work breakdown structure deliverable-oriented and thereby focus on physical deliverables that generate customer value and through which progress can be measured.

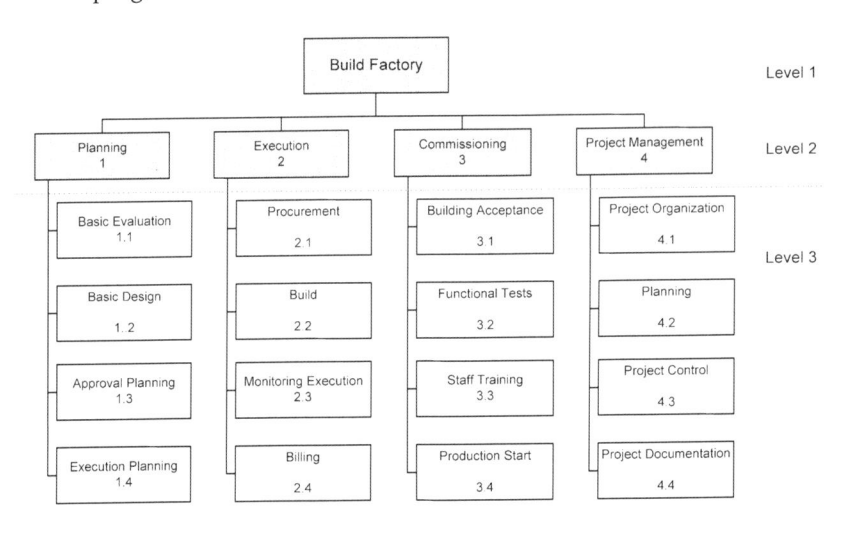

```
                          Build Factory                              Level 1
    ┌──────────────┬──────────────┬──────────────┐
  Planning      Execution    Commissioning   Project Management      Level 2
     1              2              3                4
  Basic          Procurement   Building         Project
  Evaluation        2.1        Acceptance       Organization
     1.1                          3.1              4.1                Level 3
  
  Basic Design     Build      Functional Tests   Planning
     1.2            2.2            3.2              4.2
  
  Approval       Monitoring    Staff Training   Project Control
  Planning       Execution         3.3              4.3
     1.3            2.3
  
  Execution       Billing     Production Start  Project
  Planning          2.4            3.4          Documentation
     1.4                                            4.4
```

Figure 17: The task-oriented WBS for a factory plant

Basic Concept for the Work Breakdown Structure

If the work breakdown structure is part of the contract, you should first clarify what requirements the client has to the work breakdown structure. American government departments define exactly how the Contract Work Breakdown Structure (CWBS) has to appear. For construction projects in Germany, for example, the phases are according to HOAI, the trades according to DIN 267 or the construction lots according to tender binding structures for the project. Further, company-specific guidelines are to be consulted. As a basis for the work breakdown structure, the project content/scope (Scope of Work) is used, the requirement specification or the order of the contractor. It is important that the work breakdown structure defines the total scope of the project. Everything that the WBS does not contain is not part of the project.

The Work Breakdown Structure and Earned Value Management

By now you have seen what a work breakdown structure is, what function it has and how it is built up. What special significance does the WBS now have for Earned Value Management?

If you want to implement EVM, then you can no longer afford to work without a WBS because without a clearly defined project scope and a derived work breakdown structure, it is not possible to define a clear performance measurement baseline for the application of Earned Value Management. In contrast to traditional project management, which usually monitors only the two components schedule and cost, in Earned Value Management with the additional monitoring of project scope, or the finished work, you obtain a much more comprehensive understanding of the project's progress and the health of the project.

The WBS is the most important product when it comes to defining and monitoring the project. If the WBS is not built up correctly or does not contain the entire project scope, then the used Earned Value Management System (EVMS) will not provide the correct values and is therefore useless. Without a complete WBS, as a project manager you will lose control of the project before it has even begun.

In Earned Value Management, the WBS provides the structure for:

- gathering and defining 100% of the project scope
- decomposing the project scope in defined and manageable work packages
- defining of project monitoring units (*Control Accounts*)
- budgeting and scheduling of the project
- gathering of the accrued costs (*Actual Cost*) for the comparison with the planned costs (*Planned Value*)
- comparing the cost and schedule performance (CPI and SPI)
- comparing the project end costs (*Estimate at Completion*) and project end date
- reporting of project costs, progress and the EVM performance indicators to the senior management

Suggested complementary reading: Department of Defense, Standard Practice Work Breakdown Structures for Defense Materiel Items, MIL-STD-881C, 3 October 2011, MIL-STD 881C 3 Oct 11.pdf

How to Define Work Packages

As you have read in the previous section, the work breakdown structure organizes the project hierarchically into sub-projects and sub-tasks. Its branches end with the work packages, which are not further decomposed within the work breakdown structure.

The elements of a work package are called activities or tasks. The PMBOK® emphasizes particular importance that a work package is always bound to a deliverable.

Each work package is a real task within the meaning of work, in contrast to the overlying WBS-elements. This work is done by one single person or an organizational unit up to a specified time with a defined result and effort. Normally, it is work which consists of individual tasks, but from the point of view of project management, these elements do not need to be considered as separate, but can be handled as a package. For each work package, there must be a work package manager assigned. A work package can thus be considered as a "mini-project" within the project.

Work Package Content

After having defined all the work packages, then work package tasks and deliverables/results have to be planned in detail. The sum of all work package deliverables then represent the complete scope of a project. Each work package is provided with the planned values of duration, effort, verifiable results (performance), resources and quality.

As you have already read, each work package has a defined result. A work package is completed only when the result is available and has been approved by the project manager or by quality assurance. However, the approval can only be done reasonably if quality criteria are defined in the work package description.

> "Measure what is measurable, and make measurable what is not..."
> (Galileo Galilei)

The Correct Work Package Size and Duration

From work breakdown structure planning, you know that the structure of a project should be made in such detail so that units (work packages) are developed that can be scheduled and controlled. These are handed over to an organizational authority (workgroup, department or external contractor) or to a project team member for their implementation.

A too fine detailing of the project object reduces its clarity and worsens the cost-benefit ratio of project planning. A too coarse detailing increases the risk of schedule and cost overruns. The work package size should, therefore, be chosen so that the work package can be monitored safely. To ensure that the work packages have the right size, you can apply the following rules of thumb:

The 8/80-Rule

No work package should be smaller than 8 labor hours or larger than 80. This translates into keeping your work packages duration 1 to 10 days.

The Reporting Period Rule

No work package should be longer than the distance between two status points. That means that if you have a weekly status meeting, then no work packages should take longer than a week.

The "if it's Useful" Rule

As you consider whether to break work packages down further, there can be four reasons to do so:

1. The work package is easier to estimate. Smaller work packages tend to have less uncertainty leading to more accurate estimates.

2. The work package is easier to assign. Large work packages assigned to many people lose accountability.

3. Smaller work packages assigned to fewer people can give you greater flexibility in scheduling and resource planning.

4. The work package is easier to monitor. Here, the same logic applies as in the "reporting-period rule." Smaller work packages provide more comprehensible status points. This way, you obtain more precise progress reports.

Work Package Acceptance

It is important that you define clear Acceptance Criteria for each work package, such as, scope of delivery and quality criteria. Ensure that the deliverables of each work package will be formally accepted, either by a review, inspection or test. With such an acceptance, you protect yourself from surprises, anger and frustration later in the project.

The Classification of Work

So far we have defined project scope, created the work breakdown structure and specified the work packages in detail. Now, the work of the work packages will be classified. You have probably never done this before, however, this is important in Earned Value Management for progress evaluation, for calculating the Earned Values and for determining project performance. Each work package has its own characteristics; therefore, there is not one single best way to measure progress. To accommodate the different types of work, there are several accepted Methods to measure work performance. In Earned Value Management, project work is classified in three areas:

- Discrete Effort or Measurable Effort
- Apportioned Effort
- Level of Effort (LOE)

Each of these classes has one or more measurement methods available and each method has its own characteristics for how it is applied to the work.

Discrete Effort or Measurable Effort

Discrete Effort is work for a specific end product or result. It is the preferred class of work, as it can be assessed objectively. To this category of work belongs, for example, an engineering work package, which has a construction drawing as a single and specifically measurable product.

Apportioned Effort

Apportioned Effort is work that is not directly definable and measurable. It depends on the performance and progress of another specific activity. Apportioned effort is measured as a factor, e.g., 10% of another specific activity and always refers to "Discrete Effort or Measurable Effort."

An example for an Apportioned Work can be the function of quality assurance, which inspects a statistical amount of produced products.

Level of Effort (LOE)

Level of Effort (LOE) is the third and least desired Earned Value Work Classification. LOE is not directly related to a specific product. It is only measured on the basis of a defined period. LOE does not measure performance!

This work classification is reserved for "service tasks," which do not flow directly into a final product. Often, for example, one part of the work performance of the project manager is classified as Level of Effort because mostly no specific work packages are directly bound to the performance of the project manager.

It is important to know exactly what amount of LOE is contained in the Project Baseline. If it exceeds 5%, you will have big problems to measure the project performance correctly in accordance with EVM. LOE is always isolated in a separate WBS box on level 2 and never mixed with other work, e.g., Discrete Effort. In many work breakdown structures, there is a box labeled "Project Management" on the extreme right side on level 2. It is advisable to change the name of this box into "Project Management and LOE." This approach isolates LOE and prevents it from masking real performance issues which need to be addressed.

Quentin Fleming recommends: "When you measure performance on the project, measure everything, except the 'PM and LOE' work." [2]

Work Packages and Earned Value Management

It's only useful to apply Earned Value Management if all work is defined in work packages and the project team members report about time and performance on a continuous basis. Moreover, the project should include at least 50 work packages. Otherwise, the ratio between costs and benefits is unfavorable. At less than 50 work packages, the quality of the calculated Earned Value is mostly useless. Derived from this, one could calculate that Earned Value Management is reasonably applicable from about 500,000 Euros project costs - unless you define smaller work packages.

The work package size is an important point that you should consider. With work packages that are too small, reporting work for the project team will be too much effort. If work packages are too big, the project performance will tend to be measured less frequently and therefore less corrective actions are taken. If project performance is measured on a monthly basis, then the work package duration should be less than a month - about one or two weeks.

---

[2] Quentin W. Fleming and Joel M. Koppelman – The Curse of Earned Value Management ... Level of Effort – Always Quantify and Quarantine LOE, June 2002 – The Measurable News

Earned Value Management requires regular reporting of the completion degree for all work packages. Weekly reporting is also useful for large projects. You can find the reasons for this on page 120 "When shorter reporting cycles are useful." If the work packet size was chosen appropriately, then the degree of completion can be roughly estimated, for example 0% (WP not started), 50% (WP started), 100% (WP completed). With this method, you do not lose too much accuracy compared with the value of overall project performance.

An important point in defining work package content is that material (steel, screws, machinery, etc.) is separated from labor costs, in separate work packages. This makes the assessment of the Actual Costs and of the Earned Value of work packages easier because the payment and consumption, or the installation of purchased material, usually does not occur at the same time.

Control Accounts and Budgeting

Control Accounts

In the previous chapter you read how to plan the project. This chapter would also belong to project planning; however, the concept of control accounts (monitoring units) and budgeting are so special that they deserve a chapter for their own.

The basics of this chapter are unmistakably influenced by guidelines of the DoD and the U.S. military industry. At first, I was a little skeptical too, but when you are working on international projects, you will be glad to know the following. You have probably never dealt with control accounts. This should not worry you, because behind this concept, nothing extraordinary is hidden.

This chapter deals with the question: how is the project budgeted, how should it be monitored and by whom? First, you must define which units of the project should be monitored with Earned Value Management. The main purpose of Earned Value Management is project monitoring. Normally, the project is monitored using EVM not only at the top level of the WBS, but separate sub-projects or groups of major work packages are also monitored with EVM at lower WBS levels. When the data on lower levels is analyzed, the results at the top WBS level are consolidated.

The term "Control Account" is probably still strange for you. That does not matter – you will understand the concept quickly. On the following pages, you will learn all the necessary foundations for it.

On a meaningful level of the WBS, several related work packages or a sub-project are summarized to so-called Control Account Plans CAPs. Before 1996, the DoD used the term Cost Account Plan.

Control Accounts and Budgeting

A Control Account Plan is a monitoring unit in which Earned Value Performance Measurement takes place. In Figure 18, you can see the project XLE with the CAP for the subproject "design". Each element of the WBS belongs to a particular CAP. All CAPs are evaluated separately and then consolidated at the top level of the WBS.

In contrast to the Control Account Plan, a Control Account is only one point – in fact the lowest point in WBS where Earned Value Management takes place. In a figurative sense, a Control Account is the designation of an account in bookkeeping in which all project participants record their times and costs.

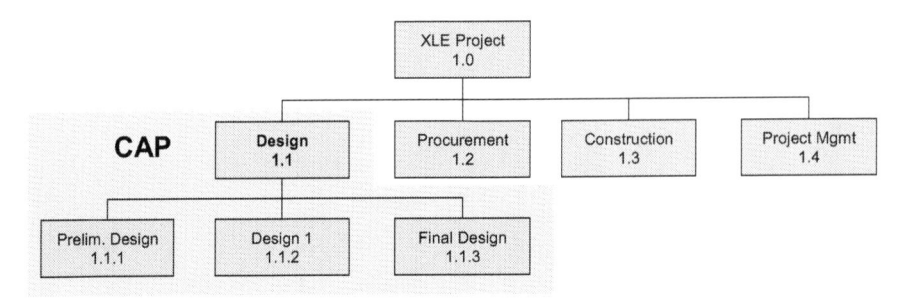

Figure 18: The Control Account Plan, the base for EVM-calculation

A Control Account includes all functions of an organization that works on the corresponding work package. It is the intersection of the Work Breakdown Structure (WBS) with the Organizational Breakdown Structure (OBS) of the company. These facts are shown in the following figure, the Responsibility Allocation Matrix (RAM).

The Control Account Manager (CAM) is a member of the functional organization and/or the project team and is responsible for his control account. That means that he manages project execution: resources, technology, time and cost aspects of his control account. He reports deviations on a weekly or monthly basis to the project manager and eventually to the functional organization. This function is usually equivalent to the sub-project manager.

The project manager sets the CAPs at defined points of the WBS. These can be at level 2, 3, 4 down to the lowest WBS level, where senior management wants to monitor the performance of a group of homogenous work during project execution. These can also be risky work packages or a large package of purchased components.

In the CAPs, the EVM performance figures, such as the Cost and Schedule Performance Index (CPI and SPI), are then calculated. These performance figures will show the senior management very quickly wherever larger deviations require actions.

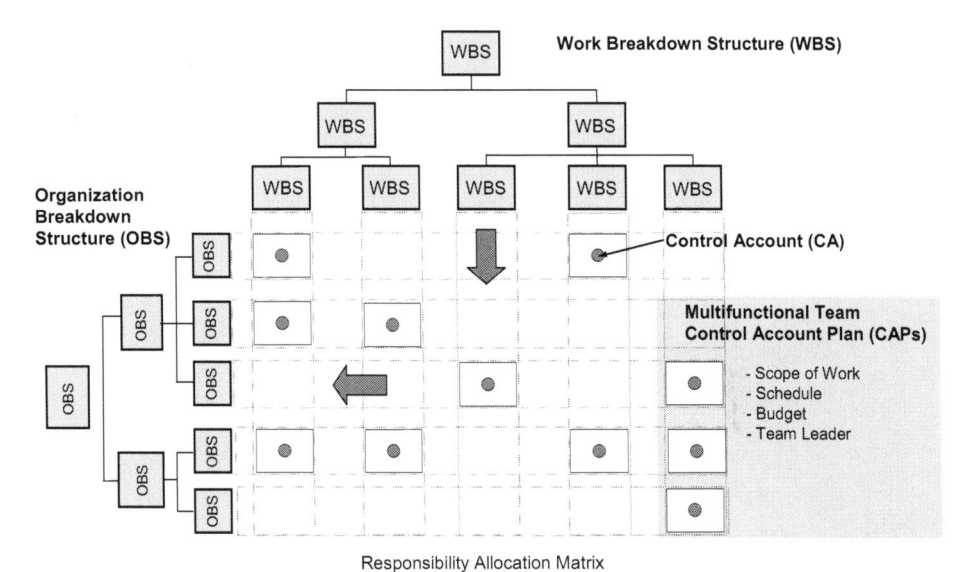

Figure 19: Responsibility Allocation Matrix with Control Accounts

When using CAPs for Earned Value Performance Measurement, the following points are important:

- All project work (scope of work) is detailed in the WBS as work packages.
- The schedule for the completion of all work packages is defined.
- The resources are approved and the budget confirmed.
- For each Control Account, one responsible person (Control Account Manager CAM) is defined.

Control Accounts and Budgeting

Each CAP is a separate monitoring cell. To be evaluated, it requires certain elements.

Typical elements of a Control Account Plan (CAP) are:

- Statement of Work
- Planning (start/end date for each work package)
- Budget (in dollars, hours or units)
- Responsible person (Control Account Manager)
- Responsible department(s) or project team members
- Type of work (one-time or periodically)
- Subdivision into individual work packages
- Used method to measure the Earned Value (e.g. 50/50 EV method, 0/100 EV method, etc.)

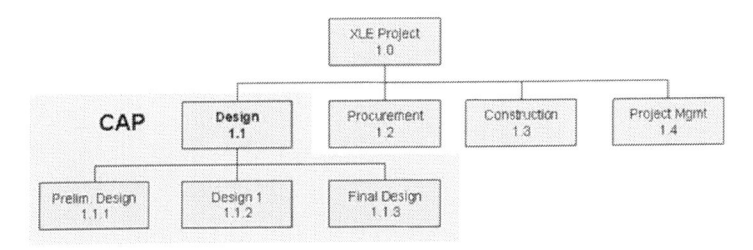

Nr.	Work Package	Resp.	EV Tech.	Item	Jan	Feb	Mar	Apr	May	BAC
1.1.1	Prelim. Design	JM	0/100	Planned	80					80
				Earned						
				Actual						
1.1.2	Design I	JM	Percent-Complete w MS Gate	Planned		200	200	100		500
				Earned						
				Actual						
1.1..3	Final Design	PH	50/50	Planned				75	75	150
				Earned						
				Actual						
1.1	Total CAP	-	-	Planned	80	200	200	175	75	730
				Earned						
				Actual						

Figure 20: Simple Control Account Plan with planned budgets and implemented EV method

Figure 20 shows schematically an example of a simple CAP with 3 work packages. Each work package in the table has a separate row for the Planned Value, Earned Value and Actual Cost. The three work packages of the CAP use three different valuation methods (EV methods), with which the degree of completion is determined and project performance is planned and measured.

Because of the short period of time, work package 1.1.1 uses the "0/100 EV Method." In work package 1.1.2, a combination of the "Percent Completed EV Method" with milestones was chosen. The work package manager estimates the degree of completion of his work package on the respective reporting dates. The first value of 200 can only be credited as Earned Value, if certain deliverables are developed and approved and thus the milestone is reached. In this example, the time duration is chosen to be quite short. In practice, this method is used for longer periods of time with defined deliverables. In work package 1.1.3, the "50/50 EV Method" was chosen. It is very suitable for estimating the degree of completion for projects with few work packages, as it evaluates empirically the progress of all work packages relatively correctly. What the EV Methods exactly mean, you will learn in detail in the next chapter.

To determine the appropriate size of CAPs, there are no guidelines. A CAP may include a work package or even a sub-project. It is important that the CAPs are homogeneous, meaningful and can be managed as a whole.

In the early days of Earned Value Management, each WBS element was assigned to a single function in the business organization. In billion dollar projects, this led to more than one thousand CAPs. With time, one has realized that it is more useful and efficient to summarize a larger quantity of homogeneous work at a higher WBS level. This is useful, as long as the relationship between the performed work and the budget is maintained. The trend today is more likely to have larger CAPs, which support the cooperation in multifunctional teams and don't need a lot of project effort.

Budgeting in Earned Value Management

In previous chapters, you saw how the project was planned using the following steps:

1. Defining the work to be performed (project scope)
2. Defining how the work is structured and monitored (work breakdown structure)
3. Assigning responsibilities to work packages and Control Account Plans
4. Project scheduling, time and resource planning (not described)

In this chapter, you will learn what the budgeting process in the Earned Value Management environment looks like. The budgeting process is a tool for the development and monitoring of cost targets for all contractually authorized work.

One of the key factors in the definition of the Earned Value Management System is that all components of the project are defined in a baseline. The main components of the Earned Value Management System are project scope, schedule and cost. In order to measure project progress, the performance is compared in terms of cost and schedule periodically with the defined baseline.

The Elements of the Contract Baseline

Once you assign defined budgets to the planned work, the Performance Measurement Baseline (PMB) is created. It is a consolidation of the budgets of all work packages, planning packages and undistributed budgets over the timeline. Based on these PMB, the current performance of the project is measured. The following figure corresponds to the usual distribution of budgets in Earned Value Management as it is applied by the DoD, DOE and their subcontractors.

At first glance, the concept might appear a bit complicated to you – however, it can be implemented in a similar way without any problems in other organizations and countries. I recommend you to take over at least the elements below the Total Allocated Budget (TAB). The following is a description of all elements of the Contract Baseline.

Total Allocated Budget (TAB)

The TAB is a very confusing concept in the Earned Value Management because its definition changes when the project or the contractual relationships further develop.

The TAB is the sum of all approved budgets allocated to the performance of the contractual effort. The TAB must always represent the Contract Budget Base (CBB) or an Over Target Baseline (OTB), if one is approved. The description for the CBB and the OTB can be found on the following pages.

The TAB is equal to the contract price minus profit/fee. It includes the entire authorized Negotiated Contract Cost (NCC), including the Authorized Unpriced Work (AUW). The AUW is the estimated cost (excl. profit/fee) for approved contract changes which, it should be noted, are still under negotiation. Herein, it is important to distinguish between costs and price. The price includes the profit/fee, but not the cost. Earned Value Management always sets in on the cost level.

```
No Over Target Baseline
TAB=CBB=NCC+AUW

With Over Target Baseline
TAB=OTB=CBB+Overrun
```

Total Contract Price
├── Total Allocated Budget (TAB)
│   ├── **Performance Measurement Baseline (PMB)**
│   │   ├── Summary Level Planning Packages
│   │   ├── Distributed Budget
│   │   │   ├── Control Accounts
│   │   │   │   ├── Work Packages
│   │   │   │   └── Planning Packages
│   │   └── Undistributed Budget
│   └── Management Reserve (MR)
└── Profit/Fee

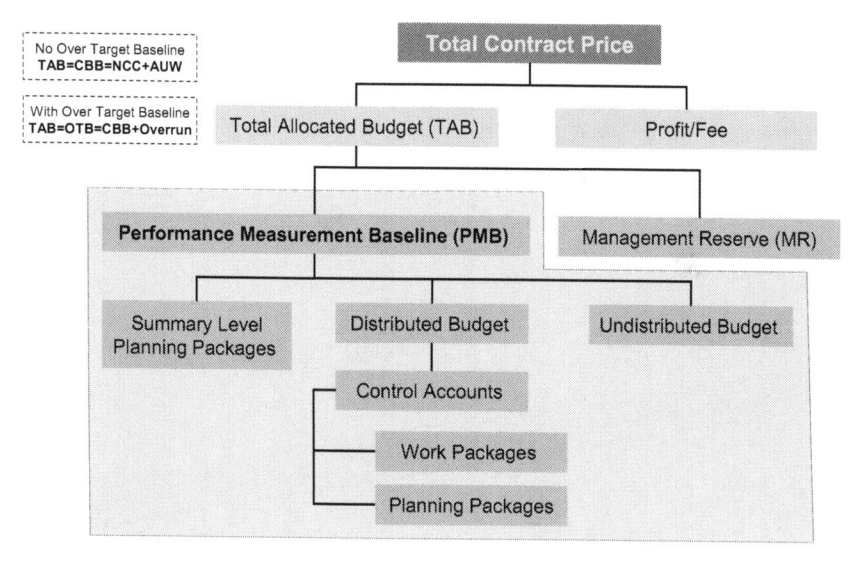

Figure 21: The elements of the Contract Baseline when budgeting the project

Negotiated Contract Cost (NCC)

The NCC is the cumulative cost (excl. profit/fee) for the original contract including all negotiated contract changes which have occurred since the beginning of the contract. The NCC is equal to the TAB if no AUW or OTB is defined.

Contract Budget Base (CBB)

The CBB is the sum of the Negotiated Contract Cost (NCC) and the Authorized Unpriced Work (AUW). This is equal to the TAB if no Over Target Baseline (OTB) is defined.

Over Target Baseline (OTB)

The OTB can be described as "recovery budget," as a new baseline. An OTB will be defined when the original defined goals cannot be achieved with the original budget. The senior management must then adapt the project goals to the new budget. A formal "reprogramming" with a new baseline is then often the last means to control the project properly again. The OTB exceeds the original target cost and requires the approval of the customer.

The OTB is the formally adjusted Total Allocated Budget (TAB), which was complemented by the additional performance measurement budget. For this reason, the OTB exceeds the contract target cost. The OTB corresponds to the contract budget base with the addition of all additional performance measurement budgets. The OTB is caused by an extra budget, either for planned work in the future, work in progress and/or for an adjustment of cost and/or schedule variance. The Total Allocated Budget is equal to the Over Target Baseline.

A reprogramming, which makes a OTB necessary

- does not result in a change of the contract
- does not change the Contract Target Cost (CTC)
- does not change the Contract Budget Base (CBB)
- does change the Performance Measurement Baseline (PMB) with prior customer's consultation

Authorized Unpriced Work (AUW)

The AUW is the estimated cost (excl. profit/fee) for approved contract changes, whose cost will still be negotiated.

Profit/Fee

The contractor receives this amount either as a fixed amount or a variable amount, depending on specific performance, cost or quality goals.

Performance Measurement Baseline (PMB)

The PMB is a central term in Earned Value Management. It is the sum of all Summary Level Planning Package (SLPP), Control Accounts (CA) and Undistributed Budget (UB), exclusive the Management Reserve (MR). The PMB is the scheduled budget, in which project performance is measured with the Earned Value management performance figures.

Summary Level Planning Package (SLPP)

A SLPP is a budget on a high level of the WBS. It is intended for identified, specific project scope, which is scheduled, but cannot be clearly assigned to control account yet. The SLPP is no substitute for an early definitive planning and should therefore be broken down as early as possible and assigned to a control account.

Undistributed Budget (UB)

The UB is intended for contractual performances or negotiated contract changes, which are only roughly defined so far and can still not be clearly assigned to the WBS or a control account. The UB is not yet scheduled. The UB should be assigned as soon as possible to a WBS element and a control account.

Management Reserve (MR)

In many projects, in particular in Research & Development projects, greater uncertainty regarding scheduling, cost estimation, technical project scope and other aspects are present. The MR is provided for unexpected problems, i.e., for those that were not recognized in risk identification, but occurred during the course of project. It is not intended for project or contract changes.

Once the Contract Budget Base (CBB) is set, the project manager defines a Management Reserve. The MR is not part of the Performance Measurement Baseline. Transactions in or out of the MR require the approval of the project manager or very often at a higher management level. A more detailed description of the Management Reserve can be found on page 66.

Distributed Budget

The Distributed Budget corresponds to the contractually authorized work, which is assigned to the WBS elements or the Control Accounts.

Control Account

A Control Account is located at the lowest point in the WBS, where Earned Value Management or performance measurement takes place. It is the focal point for the integrating and monitoring of project scope, budget, cost and schedule. Control Account budgets include one or more work packages (near focus) and planning packages (far focus).

A control account is a major management control point for:

- Cost Summarization
- Variance Analysis and Reporting
- Responsibility Assignment
- Scope Description
- Corrective Action Planning

More detailed information about Control Accounts can be found at Page 55.

Planning Packages

Planning Packages reflect a future segment of work within a Control Account that is not yet broken down into detailed work packages.

A planning package has a firm budget, estimated start and completion dates, and a statement of work. As work becomes more clearly defined, planning packages are converted into work packages.

Work Packages

A Work Package (WP) is the smallest, not further broken down element in the Work Breakdown Structure, which can be located on any WBS level. Each work package represents a real task within the meaning of work in contrast to the overlying WBS elements.

A work package describes a self-contained task within the project. The work is accomplished by a single person, a small team or an organizational unit until a specified date with a defined result and cost.

Budget Adjustments at Project Changes

For many projects, changes in project scope or specification are time sensitive. If changes occur, the responsible person, e.g., the contract-officer, will enact a so-called *Undefinitized Change Order* or *Authorized Unpriced Work* (AUW). This allows the contractor to start working, while negotiations on the changes are still held. At this date, the Total Allocated Budget (TAB) is equal to the Contract Budget Base (CBB), which corresponds to the Negotiated Contract Cost (NCC) plus the Authorized Unpriced Work. As soon as the changes are negotiated, the NCC, the CBB and the TAB are back on the same state.

For some projects, cost growth or cost overruns can reach a point where negotiations about the contract cost will be meaningless. At this date, an Over Target Baseline (OTB) will be defined. The Total Allocated Budget is now equal to the Over Target Baseline. The definition of an OTB does not change the negotiated Contract Cost or the Contract Budget Base.

The PMB - for the DoD a Significant Base for EVM

For the DoD, the development of a PMB is one of the most important aspects of Earned Value Management. This step is the base of project planning. Therefore, the DoD is willing to pay additional costs, especially at high-risk projects to demand Earned Value Management in a corresponding degree of detail.

According to the DoD, the following phases are present in the development of the PMB:

- Defining of project scope and the decomposition into manageable work packages
- Determining the relationships between the tasks between/within the work packages as well as its scheduling in a logical network
- Classifying of the work to distribute budgets
- Scheduling of the control account and work package budgets

Management Reserve/Contingency Reserve

Reserves and Buffers do not always have the best reputation - especially in senior management. This is partly understandable, because they are often hidden and not clearly identified. Herein, reserves that are properly used are a very useful tool as security for project risks.

Reserves are a time and/or cost amount, which are added to the project because of project risks. The Management Reserve (MR) in Earned Value Management is part of the approved but retained project or contract budget. It does not form part of the PMB. The MR is a budget for unexpected work. It serves as safety for risks that were not identified in the risk analysis. If these risks occur, they very often cause unexpected problems, which mean extra work for the project. For identified risks, Contingency Reserves are created which are often assigned to their own work package in the WBS. The MR budget is only for work that is within the defined project scope. Reserves are not intended for an additional project scope.

If during project execution unexpected work is identified, then a part of the MR budget is allocated to this work. Unexpected work does not mean work that needs more time, but work that was not known at the time of planning. The newly allocated budget to this work is now part of the Performance Measurement Baseline (PMB), which is used for measurement and monitoring of costs and time.

The Management Reserve is exposed openly and clearly and is not some hidden buffer. Many of you will now say this is the first position that the senior management eliminates from the budget. Therefore, it is often determined that the Management Reserve is controlled by the customer or the senior management. It will only become part of the Performance Measurement Baseline if it is effectively distributed. The status of reserves should be communicated periodically, openly and honestly – either in the periodic status report or in a line graph as shown in Figure 22.

The management reserve is usually calculated as a percentage of the total project costs and is between 2 and 15%. The size depends on the defined Contingency Reserve for identified risks and on the effort that has been dedicated to the risk analysis. That means, the better the risk level of the project is understood and the more effort that was made on a detailed risk analysis, the lower the Management Reserve can turn out.

Control Accounts and Budgeting

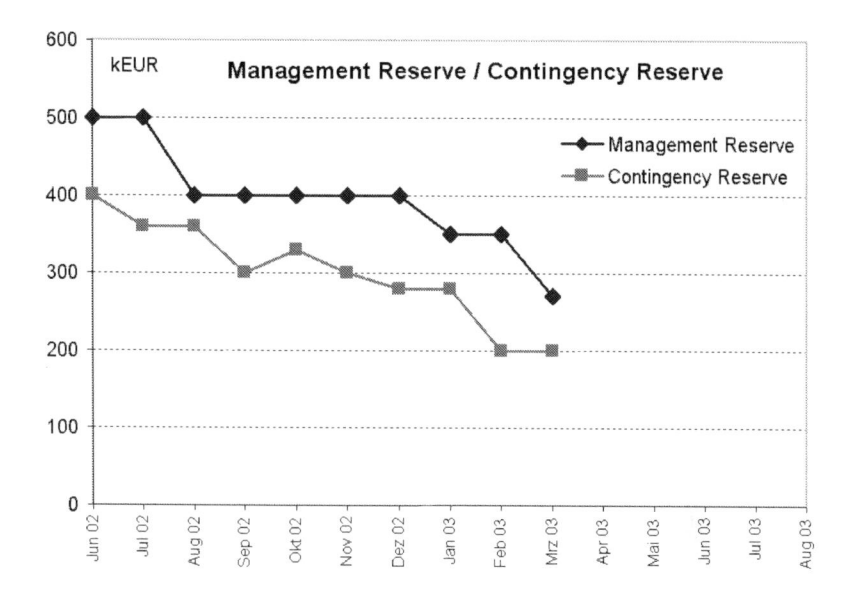

Figure 22: Management and Contingency Reserve over time

Schedule Reserve

The Schedule Reserve is similar to the Management Reserve. It is a preplanned time based reserve in the project plan, either at critical points in the network diagram, e.g., where deliveries from several work packages are to be expected, or at major milestones. The Schedule Reserve may also be placed as a safety buffer at the end of the project. Just like the Management Reserve, the Schedule Reserve is also communicated clearly and is controlled by the senior management.

However, the time buffer (*slack*) is the duration of delay of an activity or work package, without affecting the total project duration.

The following figure shows the Management Reserve and Schedule Reserve in the context of the total project cost (*Total Allocated Budget TAB*) and the total project duration (*Negotiated Completion Date*). If the costs occur as planned in the project (Planned Value), then the defined budget at the beginning of the project (*Budget at Completion BAC*) will be consumed. If during the execution of the project more than the planned budget is required, or non-identified risks occur, the Management Reserve will be consumed continuously. The situation is similar to the Schedule Reserve.

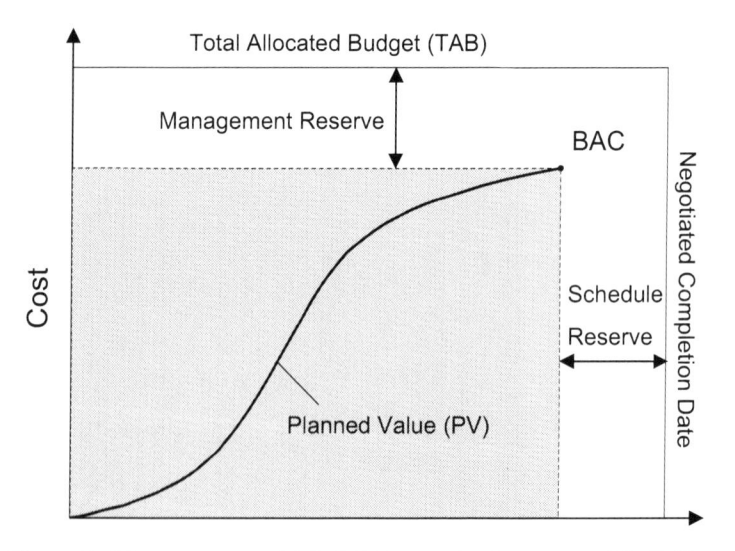

Figure 23: Management- and Schedule Reserve in the context of the TAB

Work Authorization

The authorization of work and budgets is an important part of project planning. On the one hand, the performing organizations, project team members or the Control Account Managers are sure that the work is clearly defined and dispose of an appropriate budget. On the other hand, the project manager is sure to dispose of the defined resources that perform the project work according to the schedule.

"What is the benefit of clearly defined work packages, when no one feels responsible for them?"

With the approval of the project, the overall budget will also usually be approved by a member of the senior management or the steering committee. Parallel with the creation of the baseline, but no later than before starting the work, project scope, budget and the resources must be authorized by the responsible departments in the organization. For this, normally each Control Account Plan (CAP) will be assigned to the person who is responsible for the performance. Each authorized work must be connected to a corresponding budget. At the same time, the project manager of an external contractor is granted the authorization to start the work.

After work authorization, changes of the Baseline or the Control Accounts can only be approved through the project's formal Change Control Process.

The authorization of project schedule, work, budgets and resources is performed in each project in some way – verbally or in writing. Often, only little attention is paid to this point – until resources are missing that one has scheduled but not explicitly discussed. Earned Value Management attaches great importance to the clear allocation and approval of budgets and resources. With a bit of "formalism," problems in the organization can be reduced to a great extent.

Work-Authorization Documents

The Work Authorization Document (WAD) authorizes and documents responsibilities and competencies within the specified time schedule, budget and statement of work for persons or organizations that work on the project. No work is performed without a corresponding WAD.

The WAD has the following characteristics:

- It is a mini contract for the control account between the PM and the CAM
- It clearly specifies:
    - Scope of work (WBS, descriptions)
    - Schedule (Start/End, milestones)
    - Budget (Dollars and/or units)
- It shows required interfaces to other Control Accounts

The planning process is complete when all work authorization documents were assigned and accepted.

The concept of the Control Accounts, the special budgeting and the authorization of baseline planning may seem elaborate and strange to you. However, it is more or less common practice, especially in large projects, in the Anglo-Saxon countries, the DoD, DOE and the defense industry, where EVM is mainly used. Nevertheless, the whole thing is only half as bad. Adjust EVM to the needs of your project or your company. This is no problem if you do it systematically and do not have to stick to rules of an external customer.

Earned Value Management Basis Performance Figures

New EVM-Standard – New EVM Terms

In 1996, the EVMS criteria, which were taken over from the DoD Manual 5000.2R, were revised. Then in May 1998 these were declared as national standard by the American Standards Institute/Electronic Industries Association (NSIA/EIA). From this, the standard ANSI/EIA-748 "Earned Value Management System (EVMS)" arose, which was then also taken over by the DoD. With this standard, the terms of the EVM basis performance figures were also changed.

- BCWS was renamed in PV (Planned Value)
- BCWP was renamed in EV (Earned Value)
- ACWP was renamed in AC (Actual Cost)

In 2000, the new EVM terms were incorporated into the PMBOK® of the PMI. The PMBOK® of the PMI is recognized by the ANSI as the standard ANSI/PMI 99-001-2013. However, the DoD and therefore its many large contractors still have great difficulties forgetting about the old EVM terms and applying the new ones. Therefore, you will often come across the former terms.

PV – Planned Value

The previously common term for the Planned Value was:

> BCWS – Budgeted Cost of Work Scheduled

At all times during the project, the Planned Value describes the budgeted costs of the planned work. It can only be determined from project planning. That means that it has a direct relation to the WBS. This means:

- Planned WBS $ = Planned Value $
- No WBS = No Planning = No Planned Value

The PV is the defined Baseline on which current project progress is measured. If this base has been defined, it will only be changed if adjustments of the project scope are necessary and authorized.

When you apply the Planned Value over the time course of the project, you obtain the cost plan (tabular representation), the cost trend (histogram over time) or the cost baseline (cumulative costs over time).

EV – Earned Value

The previously common term for the Earned Value was:

BCWP – Budgeted Cost of Work Performed

The Earned Value is the value of the work performed at a given time based on the planned (budgeted) value for this work. Assessing the project according to the Earned Value means to not evaluate it according to the Actual Costs, but according to the planned costs.

AC – Actual Cost

The previously common term for the Actual Cost was:

ACWP – Actual Cost of Work Performed

The Actual Cost corresponds to the actual incurred and recorded costs for the performed work up to the status date. The Actual Costs mostly derive from the accounting system of the company. Depending on the reporting cycle of the project team members and the payment of supplier invoices, the Actual Cost may be overstated or understated. For larger balances, an evaluation adjustment has to be applied.

BAC – Budget at Completion

The Budget at Completion (BAC) is an important element in the calculation of the Earned Value and the end costs of the project. The BAC correspond either to the defined total budget for the program, the project, the Control Account or Work Package. The sum of the BAC's, e.g. all work packages, is the BAC of the project. If a work package is completed, the

Earned Value Management Basis Performance Figures

Planned Value of the Work Package corresponds to the BAC of the Work Package.

The BAC is not an EVM basis performance figure, but it is described here, because we need it in the following chapter.

Overview of the EVM Performance Figures and Formulas

In the figure below, and in the following table on the next page, you will find the most important EVM Performance Figures with the corresponding formulas.

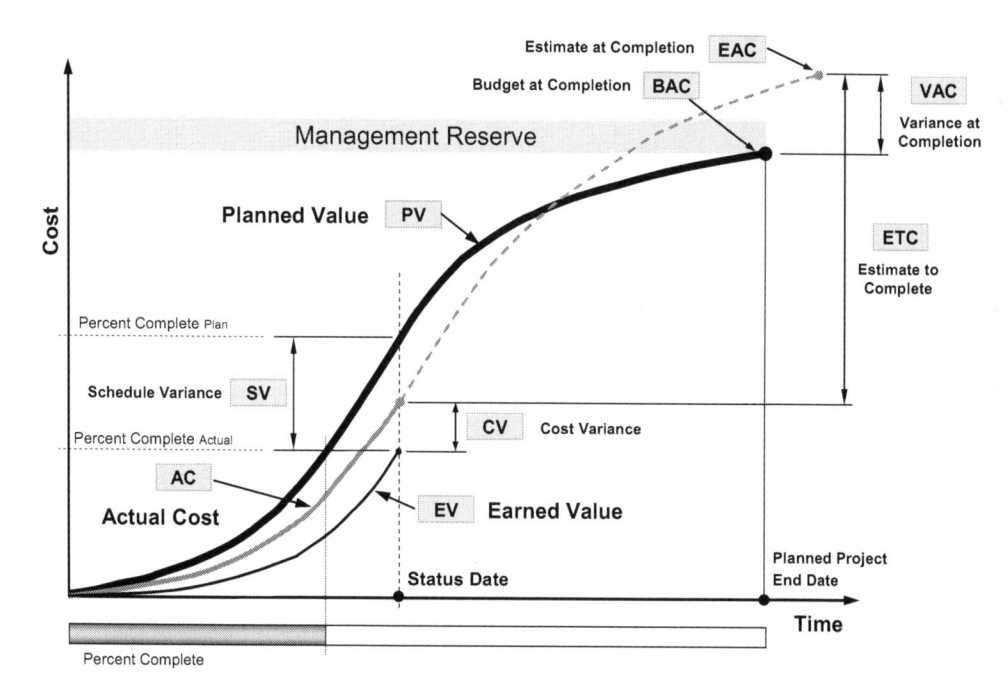

Figure 24: The EVM Performance Figures at a Glance

Earned Value Management Basis Performance Figures

Abbr.	Definition
EV (BCWP)	**Earned Value** (Budgeted Cost of Work Performed)
PV (BCWS)	**Planned Value** (Budgeted Cost of Work Scheduled)
AC (ACWP)	**Actual Cost** (Actual Cost of Work Performed)
BAC	**Budget at Completion**
SPI	**Schedule Performance Index** SPI=EV/PV (SPI=BCWP/BCWS)
CV	**Cost Variance** CV=EV-AC (CV=BCWP-ACWP)
CPI	**Cost Performance Index** CPI=EV/AC (CPI=BCWP/ACWP)
SV	**Schedule Variance** SV=EV-PV (SV=BCWP-BCWS)
EAC	**Estimate at Completion** EAC=AC+((BAC-EV)/CPI) additional variations see page 94
VAC	**Variance at Completion** VAC=(BAC-EAC)
TCPI	**To Complete Performance Index** $TCPI_{BAC}$=(BAC-EV)/(BAC-AC) or $TCPI_{EAC}$=(BAC-EV)/(EAC-AC)
ETC	**Estimate to Complete** ETC=(BAC-EV)/CPI additional variations see page 100
%	**Percent Complete**

The Calculation of the Earned Value

This is the Earned Value

The Earned Value is easiest to equate with the physical progress of the project. As the term already explains, something was earned through a certain effort. The Earned Value can be defined as follows:

Earned value is the value of the performed work at a certain time, based on the planned (budgeted) value for this work.

To determine the Earned Value of the project or a work package, various methods are used. These methods are based either on objective criteria or on subjective estimates. The significance of the Earned Value will be greatly determined by the used Earned Value Method.

The Earned Value Methods described in this book are used by the DoD (U.S. Department of Defense), DOE (U.S Department of Energy) and by other well-known Anglo-Saxon companies in the defense industry and in large engineering companies for many years. In recent years, however, they are applied more and more in several industries worldwide.

The Evaluation of Work Performance

For a reliable determination of work performance of an entire project, a detailed project planning and a concurrent calculation is required. The higher the schedule risk, the more important the correct determination of the work performance. Widely used methods for this are the three rough Earned Value estimation methods 0/100, 20/80 and 50/50. You will learn about these methods in detail on the following pages. With enough detailed project planning, it is not important which method you use to determine work performance. Crucial for the significance is the correct decomposition of project scope into controllable not long-lasting work packages.

The determination of work package performance is a challenge for many project managers and work package managers:

- The remaining effort is greatly underestimated.
- The already completed work is overrated.
- Future difficulties are not recognized or suppressed.
- Already occurred deadline overruns are played down.
- Urging by the project manager affects the "realism" of the project team member.
- Not infrequently, for a remaining effort of 10% up to 40% of the development time is required.

Especially when developing software products, estimating the percent complete is particularly difficult because software are intangible products.

EV Methods to Evaluate Work Performance

Objective Estimates are Better than Subjective Ones

The easiest way to determine work progress is to let your work package manager estimate it. He will then tell you that the work package is completed 78%. Now, how does your work package manager obtain that number? Probably, he has subjectively estimated it. Such subjective estimates are very uncertain, especially at work packages with longer duration. As project manager, I myself often overestimate work progress of work packages and underestimate the remaining work. Are you the same way? For this reason, objective methods for the determination of work performance are used in Earned Value Management. The reason also provides the following saying:

> "The same work under the same conditions will be estimated differently by ten different estimators or by one estimator at ten different times."

To evaluate work progress of a work package, several Earned Value Methods can be used. They have a large impact on the significance of the Earned Value.

Which Earned Value Method is used to determine the Earned Value, depends on the work package content, the type of work, the used resources and especially the work package duration. Work packages, which are at the status date still in progress and are not completed in one single report-

The Calculation of the Earned Value

ing period, demand special requirements. In this case, it is often useful to define specific milestones and interim results within the work package in order to facilitate the determination of work progress. This reduces the risk of wrong estimations in a subjective evaluation.

EV Methods are divided into three main groups, depending on the type of defined work:

- Earned Value Methods for Discrete Effort or Measurable Effort
    - Percent Start/Percent Finish EV Method (50/50), (25/75), (80/20)
    - Percent Start/Percent Finish EV Method (0/100)
    - Percent-Complete EV Method
    - Weighted Milestones EV Method
    - Weighted Milestones with Percent-Complete EV Method
    - Units Completed EV Method (Physical Measurement)
- Apportioned Effort EV Method
- Level of Effort EV Method (LOE)

On the following pages, you will learn in detail about the most important EV methods. You will learn how the Earned Value and the Planned Value is determined in the individual EV methods. You will find a detailed description of the Earned Value and Planned Value starting on page 71.

Percent Start/Percent Finish EV Method 50/50, 25/75, 80/20

The "Percent Start/Percent Finish EV Method" (also known as "Fixed Formula Method") is bound to the start and end of a work package. It is an objective method because the project team member has no influence on the calculation of the degree of completion. With this, one wants to prevent a too positive statement about project progress being made by estimating the degree of completion.

The described EV Methods can be visualized using a simple Control Account with five work packages. When evaluating work performance, the Planned Value and Earned Value are always determined at the status date.

50/50 EV Method

The "50/50 EV Method" is used to simplify the determination of work progress of tasks and work packages.

How to determine the Planned Value (PV): At the *planned* start of the work package, the first 50% of the BAC are credited to the PV. The second 50% are attributed at the *planned* completion to the PV. Throughout the whole period, the Planned Value does not increase. The Planned Value automatically takes the value of 100%, if the planned end date of the work package is in the past.

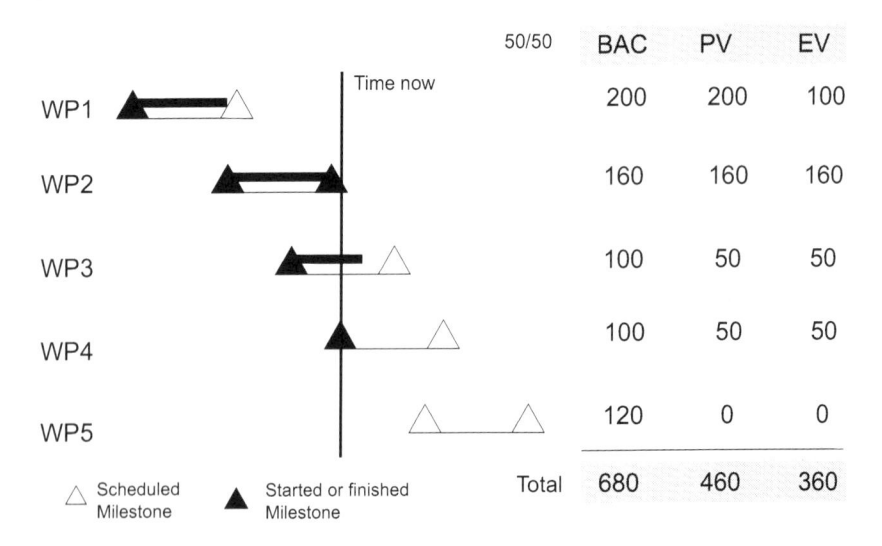

50/50	BAC	PV	EV
WP1	200	200	100
WP2	160	160	160
WP3	100	50	50
WP4	100	50	50
WP5	120	0	0
Total	680	460	360

Figure 25: Determine the Earned Value with the „50/50 EV Method

The Calculation of the Earned Value

How to determine the Earned Value (EV): For the EV, the same procedure applies as for the PV. However, the *effective* start and end of the work package are decisive for the credit note. At the *effective* start of the work package, the first 50% of the BAC will be credited as EV. During the remaining time of the work package, this value does not increase. As soon as the work package is completed, the remaining 50% of the budgeted costs are credited to the EV. The "50/50 EV Method" is essentially a compromise between the 0/100 EV Method and the estimation of the degree of completion.

In the "50/50 EV Method" performance is often overestimated in the first half of the work package duration, but underestimated in the second half. Therefore, this method should only be used for short work packages that are started and completed within two consecutive reporting periods.

0/100 EV Method

"0/100 EV Method" is a special case of the "Percent Start/Percent Finish EV Method." It is used for short work packages/activities that are completed within one reporting period.

The "0/100 EV Method" works with a very careful evaluation of the work performance. Therefore, it is unsuitable for projects with few work packages, as this can lead to significant distortions of reality. So it may happen that the total work progress has a constant value for a certain time. If several work packages are completed at the same time, there will be a large leap in work progress. However, this method is very useful for projects

	BAC	PV	EV
WP1	200	200	0
WP2	160	160	160
WP3	100	100	0
WP4	100	0	0
WP5	120	0	0
Total	680	460	160

Figure 26: Determine the Earned Value with the „0/100 EV Method"

The Calculation of the Earned Value

with many small and short work packages as well as short reporting cycles.

The "0/100 EV Method" is the most conservative EV Method to evaluate project performance, as it tends to underestimate work progress of the project. This fact makes it the safest of all EV Methods.

Percent Complete EV Method

The "Percent Complete EV Method" is a subjective EV Method. It is also called "Relative Method" or "Supervisor's Estimate." This method is used for longer work packages; however, it is not the preferred method for determining the Earned Value. In this method, the percent complete can take any value between 0 and 100. In the "Percent Complete EV Method," the Control Account Manager or the responsible person for the work package determines the Planned Value and estimates the degree of progress of work completed.

The advantages and disadvantages of this method are obvious. The estimates are only as good as the estimator himself. It is known that risks are often underestimated and that the project team, and also the project manager, is rather optimistic when it comes to estimate project progress. Therefore, according to experience, often too high values are estimated for the Percent Complete.

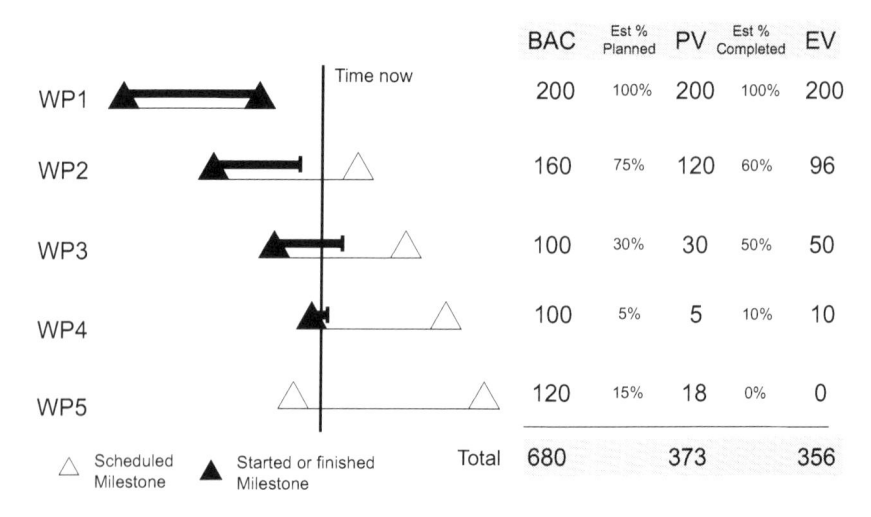

	BAC	Est % Planned	PV	Est % Completed	EV
WP1	200	100%	200	100%	200
WP2	160	75%	120	60%	96
WP3	100	30%	30	50%	50
WP4	100	5%	5	10%	10
WP5	120	15%	18	0%	0
Total	680		373		356

△ Scheduled Milestone   ▲ Started or finished Milestone

Figure 27: Determine the Earned Value with the „Percent Complete EV Method"

Weighted Milestones EV Method

The "Weighted Milestones EV Method" is a preferred objective Earned Value Method for discrete work and is especially suitable for long term work packages. With this method, at least one progress milestone should be defined for each reporting period. A milestone is a significant point or event in the project signaling the completion of a key deliverable, marking the completion of a project phase or signifying an important decision.

In the "Weighted Milestones EV Method", the Planned Value is calculated using the milestone plan and the Earned Value is bound to the accomplishment of the respective milestones. With this Earned Value Method, unfavorable cost and schedule trends will become obvious at the end of each reporting period. Thus, the progress of the project will be more transparent for customers. Milestones are tied to deliverables to be provided and for an official acceptance, even of intermediate results.

If the status date does not have the same date as a milestone, as shown in Figure 29 of Work Package 3 (WP3), the value of the Planned Value corresponds to the following milestone and the Earned Value gets the value of the already achieved milestone. This procedure meets the principle of prudence.

The "Weighted Milestones EV Method" can be manipulated despite its great advantages by giving an earlier milestone a greater weight by discounting the weight of the completion milestone. This can then be expressed in positive EVM costs performance figures. However, as one mile-

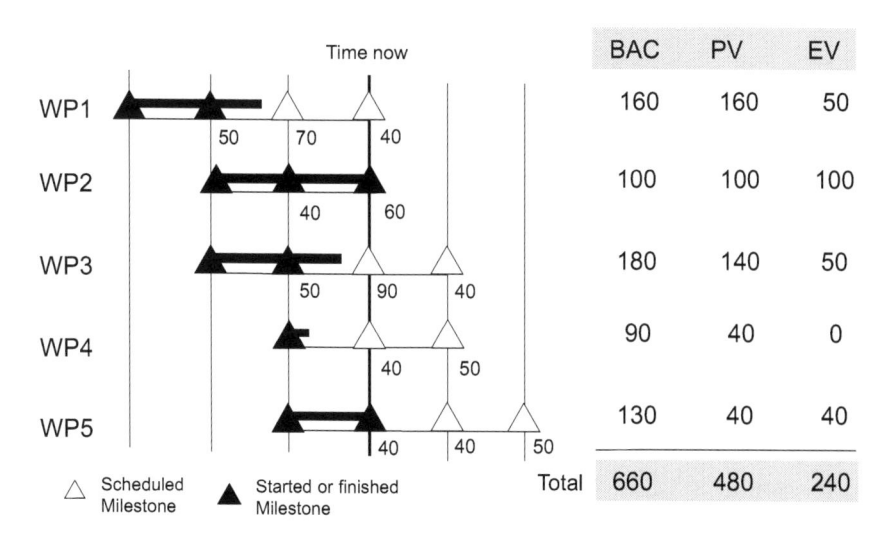

WP	BAC	PV	EV
WP1	160	160	50
WP2	100	100	100
WP3	180	140	50
WP4	90	40	0
WP5	130	40	40
Total	660	480	240

Figure 28: Determine the Earned Value with the „Weighted Milestones EV Method"

The Calculation of the Earned Value

stone is defined in each reporting period, one missed milestone always affects results in unfavorable EV schedule metrics. Despite the low risk of manipulation, the "Weighted Milestone EV Method" is the best EV Method for long term discrete work packages.

Weighted Milestones with Percent Complete EV Method

The "Weighted Milestones with Percent Complete EV Method" is a compromise between the "Weighted Milestones EV Method" and the "Percent Complete EV Method." It is suitable for long term discrete work packages with specific intermediate results.

This method includes "Percent Complete" as a subjective element. Therefore, it is less suitable than the "Weighted Milestone EV Method."

As the "Weighted Milestones with Percent Complete EV Method" tends to have fewer Weighted Milestones, the project manager has to determine the achieved planned Value and Earned Value between the milestones subjectively. At least at every second reporting period, one milestone should be defined. The more specific one defines the milestones with appropriate deliverables, the better. Just as at the "Percent Complete EV Method," the estimates are only as good as the estimator.

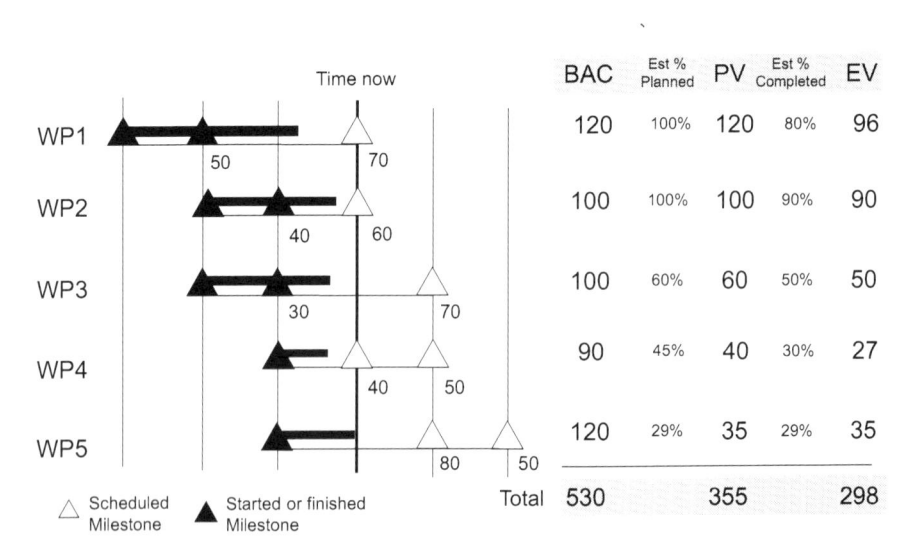

	BAC	Est % Planned	PV	Est % Completed	EV
WP1	120	100%	120	80%	96
WP2	100	100%	100	90%	90
WP3	100	60%	60	50%	50
WP4	90	45%	40	30%	27
WP5	120	29%	35	29%	35
Total	530		355		298

△ Scheduled Milestone   ▲ Started or finished Milestone

Figure 29: Determine the EV with the " Weighted Milestones with Percent Complete EV Method "

Units Completed EV Method (Physical Measurement)

The "Units completed EV Method" is a simple method for long term work packages, ideal for continuous flow processes and the mass production of noncomplex systems, where measurable or quantifiable result are produced. The Planned Value is based on the budget value of the planned units and the Earned Value on the number of actual produced units.

The table below shows a simple example with a Control Account for the production of special cables. For a power plant project, 6300 meters of cable have to be produced in the illustrated monthly amount – and this at the budgeted cost of 10 Dollars per meter. To calculate the Planned Value with this method, you only have to multiply the planned monthly production with the price per meter. The Earned Value is calculated the same way, but with the current production.

Month	April	May	June	July	Total
Planned Production	1000	1500	2000	1800	6300
Planned Value (10 $/m)	$10'000	$15'000	$20'000	$18'000	$63'000
Actual Production	800	1'600	1'900	2'000	6'300
Earned Value	$8'000	$16'000	$19'000	$20'000	$63'000

Figure 30: Control Account – Production of special cables

Apportioned Effort EV Method

The "Apportioned Effort EV Method" is an EV Method as well as a work package category. It is also called "Secondary Proportionality Method," as performance delivery and thus the degree of progress of the Control Account or work package is based on the progress of another unit. A proportional cost activity is typically a support activity or staff function which can be tied to discrete work or to a specific product, such as quality assurance in engineering, performance-accompanying audit work/documentation or assembly control proportional to the assembling. It differs from the category "Level of Effort EV Method" (*LOE*), which has no direct relation to a specific product. The "Apportioned Effort EV Method" is better than "Level of Effort," however less suitable than EV Methods for measurable work, such as the 0/100 or 50/50-EV Method.

An "apportioned effort" Planned Value is directly proportional to the associated discrete effort's budget and time phasing. An "apportioned effort" Earned Value is directly proportional to the actual amount of discrete work, that is completed during the reporting period. An advantage of this method is that it simplifies the Earned Value calculation of recurring support activities by defining standardized percentages for these tasks.

QA Control Account Apportioned at 10% of Production Control Account	Jul	Aug	Sep	Total
Production Control Account PV	300	600	200	1100
Quality Assurance Control Account PV	30	60	20	110
Production Control Account EV	250	500	350	1100
Quality Assurance Control Account EV	25	50	35	110

Figure 31: QA Control Account with Apportioned Effort

It is especially valuable when an organization is providing simultaneous direct support to numerous projects. For example, the cost for a quality assurance department has historically been ten percent of the manufacturing production cost. The obvious problem with this method is that it measures the performance of the discrete task rather than actual performance of the supporting activity. In Figure 31 you can see the application of the "apportioned effort EV Method" in a simple quality assurance control account.

Level of Effort (LOE) EV Method

Level of Effort is a subjective Earned Value Method as well as a work package category. LOE is the least desirable of all Earned Value Methods because it does not measure physical performance, but only the passage of time. LOE should be limited to general and supportive assistance activities that are not associated to any item or product. These include project office tasks including the project manager or field support engineering. The Planned Value of LOE activities are determined by allocating the control account budget across the task's period of performance. The Earned Value is then earned by the passage of time, and by its definition, will always be equal to the reporting period's Planned Value. Since the Earned Value always corresponds to the Planned Value, there is no schedule or cost variance. LOE cannot provide early warning signals or contribute anything to the prediction of the project cost.

LOE is often used out of convenience - it is simple and you do not need to think much about it. Therefore, it is important to know exactly the amount of LOE contained in the project baseline. If it exceeds 5%, you will have serious problems measuring project performance correctly in accordance with EVM. Therefore, the advice of Quentin W. Fleming is: "If you want to measure the performance of the project correctly, then measure everything except project management and LOE."[3]

Implementing EV Methods Correctly

"What EV Method should I choose for my project for evaluating work performance?" This question is often heard. "Does it make a difference whether I use the EV Method 0/100, 20/80, 50/50 or 80/20 for direct work?"

It doesn't matter which method you choose. If your project has more than 200 work packages that are not long-lasting and it is mostly worked parallel, then you will not find relevant difference in the overall degree of completion of the project. At the very beginning of every project, you still have greater inaccuracies in the overall degree of completion and the calculated performance figures. But as soon as a few weeks have passed, the inaccuracy in the overall degree of completion will be after the first decimal place.

None of the described EV Methods will be appropriate for the entire project. Each project needs several EV Methods – depending on the classification of the work, the most appropriate has to be chosen. However, you should seek to make each work identifiable, measureable and monitorable as well as to provide it with clear deliverables.

---

[3] Quentin W. Fleming and Joel M. Koppelman – The Curse of Earned Value Management ... Level of Effort – Always Quantify and Quarintine LOE, June 2002 – The Measurable News

Project Monitoring with EVM Performance Figures

CV – Cost Variance

The Cost Variance (CV) answers the question: How much are the Actual Costs of the performed work under or over the budgeted costs at the status date? The Cost Variance is calculated by subtracting the Actual Cost (AC) at the status date from the Earned Value (EV).

$$CV = EV - AC \text{ or } BCWP - ACWP$$

The Cost Variance can be expressed as a percentage by dividing the Cost Variance (CV) by the Earned Value (EV).

$$CV\% = CV/EV \text{ or } CV/BCWP$$

A negative cost variance means that the approved budget for the work performed to date has been exceeded.

SV – Schedule Variance

The Schedule Variance (SV) answers the questions: Is the project ahead or behind schedule in accomplishing the work? How much are the planned cost over or under the budget costs of work performed at the status date?

The Schedule Variance is calculated by subtracting the Planned Value (PV) from the Earned Value (EV) at the status date. A positive SV indicates that more work has been accomplished than planned. A negative SV indicates that less work has been accomplished.

$$SV = EV - PV \text{ or } BCWP - BCWS$$

The Schedule Variance can be expressed as a percentage by dividing the Schedule Variance (SV) by the Planned Value (PV).

$$SV\% = SV/PV \text{ or } SV/BCWS$$

The Schedule Variance expressed in Euros or Dollars often leads to confusion. The SV derives from accounting data and not from the "time-based planning." As the SV does not measure time, the detailed analysis of the "time-based planning" is also important – especially towards the end of the project. Although the project is behind schedule, the Earned Value will converge more and more with the Planned Value to the actual end of the project, until the difference of the two values is zero. The validity of the SV is, therefore, only useful as long as the project will be finished on or before the planned project completion date. If the planned project completion date is expected to exceed, the SV loses its significance some time before the project completion.

"Things always get better after they get worse. So it's good to make things worse as quickly as possible."

CPI – Cost Performance Index

The CPI is the cost-related performance figure. It measures the efficiency of the achieved "physical progress" compared to the baseline. The CPI is mainly used for the calculation of the estimated costs at the end of the project (Estimate at Completion EAC).

The CPI answers the question: "How efficiently are we using our resources?" It also reveals planning errors and too optimistic estimates. The CPI is calculated by dividing the Earned Value (EV) by the Actual Cost (AC).

$$CPI = EV/AC \quad \text{or} \quad BCWP/ACWP$$

With a CPI higher than 1.0, the project results were produced at a lower cost than originally planned. At a value less than 1.0, the project overdraws the budget. That means that with a CPI of 0.95, only 95 cents value (Earned Value) for every Dollar spent was realized.

The significance of the CPI is empirically proven. In a study by the DoD with more than 800 projects, one found that the CPI starts to stabilize after about 20% of project completion and, at project completion, it is only slightly worse than at 20% project completion. Therefore, the CPI can be used for predicting the final project costs (*Estimate at Completion EAC*) after only 20% of project completion. However, in complex, innovative projects, especially in R&D projects, the risk is high that the CPI continues to get worse until project completion. So it is rather unlikely that the CPI improves significantly towards the end of the project.[4]

SPI – Schedule Performance Index

The Schedule Performance Index (SPI) is the time-related performance figure of Earned Value Management. It is calculated by dividing the Earned Value (EV) by the Planned Value (PV).

$$SPI = EV/PV \quad \text{or} \quad BCWP/BCWS$$

A SPI value higher than 1.0 indicates that project results were accomplished faster than originally planned, while a value less than 1.0 means that the project is progressing too slowly. At a value of 1.0, you obtain one Dollar of Earned Value for every Dollar of planned work.

The SPI converges towards project completion always to the value 1.0, as the Earned Value then equals the Planned Value or, in other words, anything planned was also completed. The validity of the SPI is therefore only useful as long as the project will also be finished on or before the planned project completion date. If the planned project completion date is expected to be late, the SPI loses its significance some time before the project completion.

---

[4] David Christensen, Ph.D. and Carl Templin, Ph.D. – EAC Evaluation methods: Do they still work? – Acquisition Review Quarterly — Spring 2002

Graphical Representation of the CPI and SPI

In the following figure, you can see the graphical representation of the CPI and SPI. They are either shown both or separately in a diagram. Has the project achieved what was planned in the predefined time? If so, then this corresponds to the "standard project performance," which is assigned to the value 1.0.

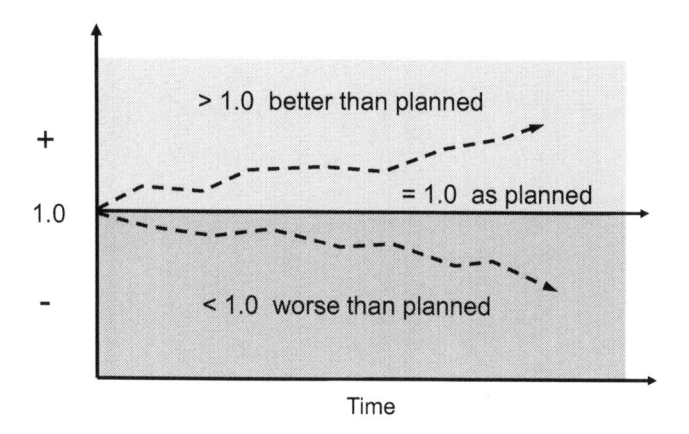

Figure 32: Graphical representation of CPI or SPI

Cumulative or current CPI, SPI?

The CPI and the SPI can be calculated and shown as cumulative or current values, e.g., the CPI of the month. In most cases, you will see the data of the cumulative values that show the trend of the performance figures or project performance better.

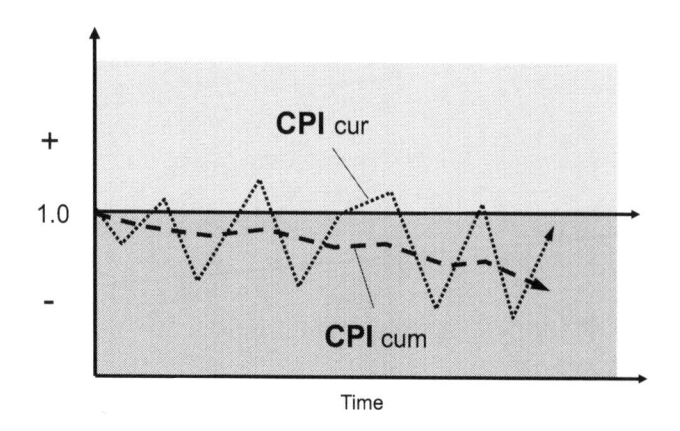

Figure 33: EVM Chart with cumulative and current CPI, SPI

The current CPI and SPI values show the performance of the work of the corresponding weeks or months. These values can be used for comparisons with previous periods.

- CPI cur = CPI current
- CPI cum = CPI cumulative

If it is not further specified which CPI or SPI it is, then you can assume that it is the cumulative one

The Behavior of SV, CV, SPI and CPI

On the previous pages, I have pointed out that the SV and SPI do not behave as the CV and the CPI. In the next two figures, you can see the behavior of SV, CV, SPI and CPI more in detail. You should really know this well; otherwise you may experience a bad surprise.

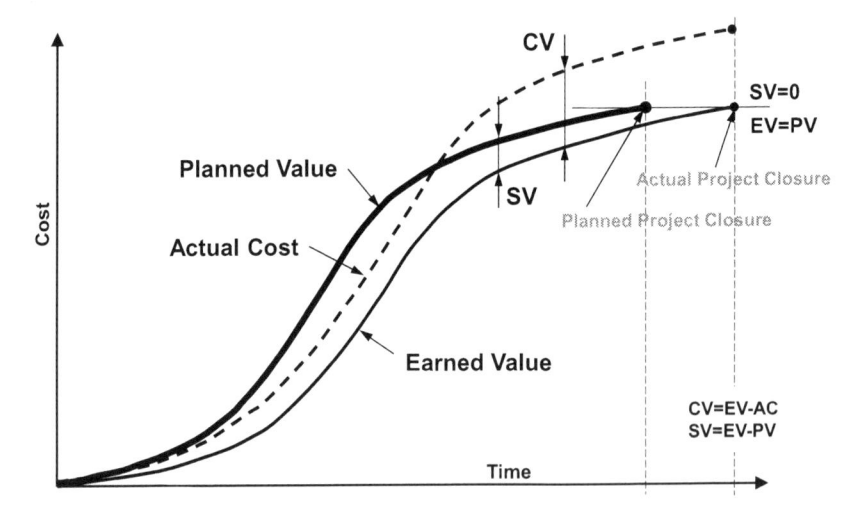

Figure 34: The Behavior of CV and SV

In Figure 34, you can see that the SV is getting smaller towards the effective end of the project and then converges to "0". This is because the EV and PV always takes on the same value at the end of the project. For this reason, the value of the SV is usually no longer useful approximately from the last quarter of the project duration. However, the CV represents the correct cost variance at any time up to the effective end of the project. Only in one case, the CV will be "0" at the end of the project, namely if the project is completed within budget - but this is rarely the case.

Now, let's look at the behavior of SPI and CPI more closely. In Figure 13 you can see that the SPI converges to "1" towards the end of the project, although the project has exceeded the costs significantly. Also, in this case, the EV and PV take on the same value at the end of the project and, therefore, the quotient of EV and PV is equal to "1". The CPI will be rarely "1" at project end – only if the project is completed within the planned costs.

The problems with the insufficient reliability of the SV and SPI were already known for a long time, but were never really tackled until the "Earned Schedule" concept, which was developed by Walter Lipke in summer of 2002 and published for the first time in March 2003. This concept has been regarded as a promising mathematical approach for time-related EVM-performance figures.

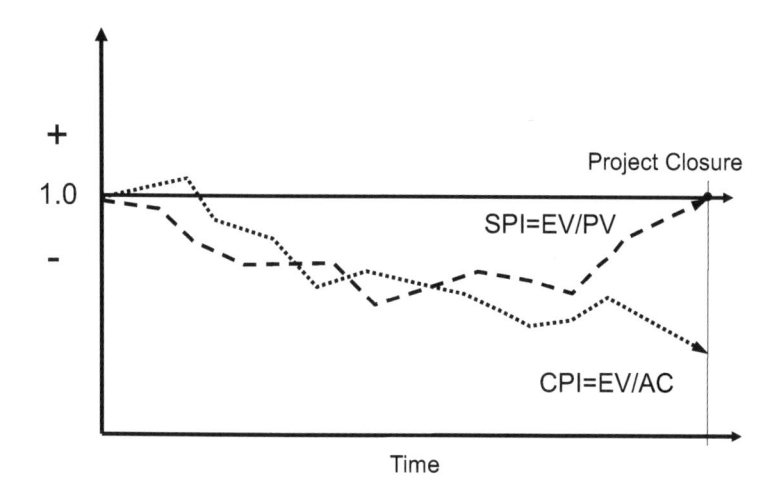

Figure 35: The Behavior of SPI and CPI

Project Forecasts

Forecasts – an Effective Management Tool

In forecasts, one makes estimates of the future status of the project, especially of costs and completion dates. With Earned Value Management, you have an excellent tool to make meaningful forecasts very early in the project life. However, there are situations during project implementation, in which you would prefer to know nothing of the future. This is also shown through Fitzgerald's first law of program management, which follows:

> *"There are only two phases to a big military program. Too early to tell and too late to stop."*

Fitzgerald wants to express the following: programs prefer to hide or to repress bad news until so much money is spent to apply the "sunk cost argument." This means that it is too late to stop the program because too much money was already spent.

This law is prevalent very real and widespread, not necessarily because of intentional withholding or misinterpretation of information, but simply due to a lack of objective and accurate information about the current status of projects and programs. Therefore, forecasts about the further course of the project or the project end costs are almost impossible. Senior management is responsible for the results of the projects. Therefore, it needs information that will allow managing projects and programs effectively. If EVM is implemented correctly, then the necessary information is available to prevent "Fitzgerald's first law of program management."

Knowing Early What the Future Will Bring

There are many reasons why more and more companies monitor their projects with Earned Value Management. One of the main reasons is the possibility of a "statistical" forecast of the probable end costs of the project and the project end date at a very early date. Already after 15% project

Project Forecasts

progress, the first forecasts can be made. With Earned Value Management you don't have to wait until 80 % of the budget is spent to know that one is heading towards a problem.

"It's tough to make predictions, especially about the future."
(Mark Twain)

Mark Twain is right with his statement. However, with Earned Value Management, the senior management has a tool that provides early warning signals and thus allows taking corrective actions on time.

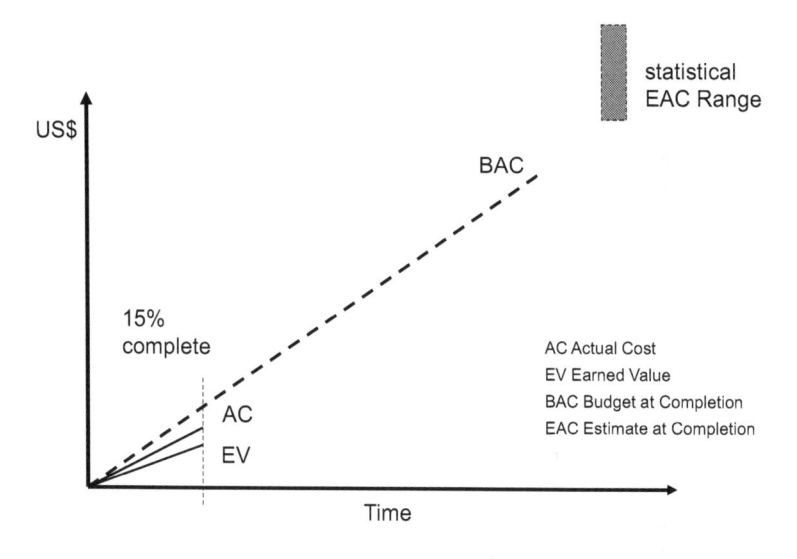

Figure 36: Early warning after 15% project progress - BAC, EV and AC

In Figure 36, you can see what is meant. For the project, a baseline was defined with a budget at completion (BAC). Even after only 15% completion, deviations can be recognized. The performed work could not stick to the plan and it took more money to complete the work. Using Earned Value Management, the project manager can make a forecast quite fast of how much resources, time and budget will probably still needed until the project completion. This way, you can get an early statistical forecast of the project end costs and the project end date.

The results should only be understood and communicated as an estimate and not as an absolute number that will definitely be reached until the end of the project. This calculation is suitable in the first place to see whether a cost or a time problem is present and if emergency measures have to be initiated.

Unfortunately, the forecasts only rarely show a good future. How many projects do you know that cost less than planned or were finished earlier than planned? The sooner you take and initiate appropriate measures, the better. With EVM, you have the possibility to initiate measures very early to prevent the project from the worst.

EAC – Estimate at Completion

Only a few projects end with the costs planned at project start - most projects cost more. Therefore, early measures have to be implemented whenever necessary to prevent uncontrolled cost growth.

> *"Tell me how your project starts and I will tell you how it will end."*

This saying applies exactly to the experience of the DoD. It has been found that from 20% of the project progress on, the percentage cost deviation does not become smaller, but tends to become larger. This has the consequence that the project end costs are probably a lot higher than planned.

In practice, for the forecast of the project end costs (*Estimate at Completion EAC*), three calculation methods are used:

- Optimistic Method *(Divisor = 1.0)*
- Realistic Method *(Divisor = CPI)*
- Pessimistic Method *(Divisor = CPI x SPI)*

The following data is required:

- The Actual Cost at the status date
- The value of the Work Remaining
- Depending on the calculation type CPI or/and SPI

The value of the Work Remaining corresponds to the budgeted value of the unfinished work packages, or the Budgeted at Completion (BAC) minus the already achieved Earned Value.

Optimistic Method (Mathematical or Overrun to Date EAC)

In the optimistic method, one assumes that all future work will be executed as budgeted. Therefore, in the formula of the following figure, the divisor 1.0 is used. Although the formula is considered as not useful, it can be used in certain cases. For example it is used if one wants to calculate the lowest possible value of the project end costs.

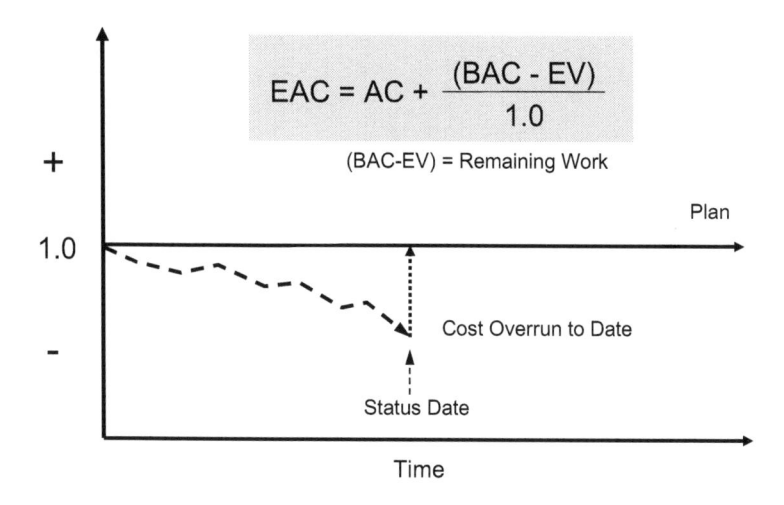

$$EAC = AC + \frac{(BAC - EV)}{1.0}$$

$(BAC-EV)$ = Remaining Work

Figure 37: Optimistic Method (Mathematical or Overrun to Date EAC)

At an early stage of the project, the first half of the project duration is certainly planned better than the second half. Therefore, it is usually unlikely that a cost overrun can be recouped during the following project duration – in particular, if at the status date more than 30…40 % of the project has been completed. In the optimistic case, the cost overrun at the end of the project will have the same value as at the status date. This case is calculated in the optimistic method.

Realistic Method (Low-End Cumulative CPI EAC)

The most often used method to calculate the project end costs is the so-called "Low-end Cumulative CPI EAC". In this method, one assumes that the future work will be carried out with the previous performance. The formula in Figure 38 is also backed by the most scientific data, which confirms the reliability of this method as a forecast tool. The DoD found that the cumulative CPI tends to stabilize already after 15 - 20% of completed project work. However, in many cases, the cumulative CPI worsens towards the end of the project period (see also the description of the CPI on page 91).

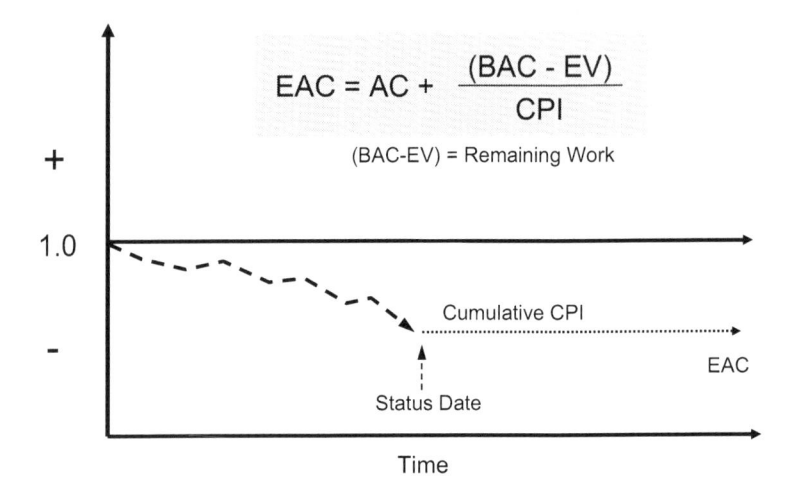

$$EAC = AC + \frac{(BAC - EV)}{CPI}$$

(BAC-EV) = Remaining Work

Figure 38: Realistic Method (Low-End Cumulative CPI EAC)

The formula above can be simplified and represented as follows: EAC=BAC/CPI. The result is the same.

The "Low-end Cumulative CPI EAC" is considered by many experts to be the formula for calculating the lowest minimum project end costs; others consider it as a forecast of the most probable end costs of the project. There may be reasons to support a better EAC. However, since 1991, the project managers of the DoD must describe precisely how they want to achieve this.

Pessimistic Method (High-End Cumulative CPI x SPI EAC)

"If you can interpret project status data in several different ways, only the most painful interpretation will be correct."

The last statistical formula takes care of the above saying and combines the Cost Performance Index with the Schedule Performance Index. There are good reasons to support this formula, which is increasingly gaining acceptance: No project manager likes it when the senior management approves of a project plan that cannot be complied after a certain time. Most project managers, of course, want to get back to the approved plan; however, this means that more resources are required to finish the same amount of work. In this case, it is often worked overtime and additional staff is employed. It is, therefore, not surprising that this very reliable CPI is nullified. Some people regard the "Cumulative CPI x SPI EAC" as the "worst-case" scenario and others as the "most probable" forecast.

The project manager will compare the calculated EAC always with its own best estimate. If his estimate is better than the statistically calculated EAC, then he should have a good explanation ready for the senior management of how he wants to achieve his estimation.

$$EAC = AC + \frac{(BAC - EV)}{CPI \times SPI}$$

(BAC-EV) = Remaining Work

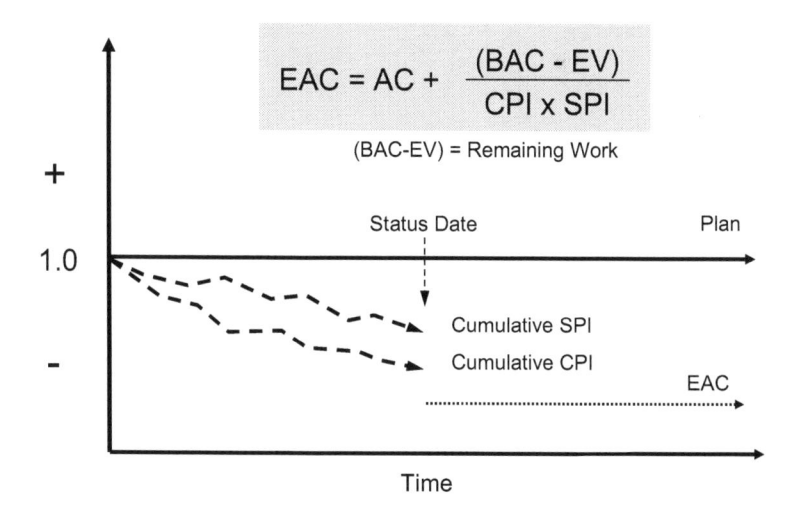

Figure 39: Pessimistic Method (High-End Cumulative CPI x SPI EAC)

VAC – Variance at Completion

The cost Variance at Completion (VAC) calculates the difference between the Budget at Completion (BAC) and Estimate at Completion (EAC) and so forecasts the amount of budget deficit or surplus at the end of the project. In EAC, you have the choice whether you want to choose the optimistic, the realistic or the pessimistic method. You can find the different methods of the EAC on page 94.

$$VAC = BAC - EAC$$

If the calculation shows a negative result, then the project has to face a budget overrun at the end of the project. This budget overrun can be represented well on a trend graphic and demonstrates immediately to the management, if towards the end of the year one can still count on a good bonus or a new company car, or if one has to tighten one's belt.

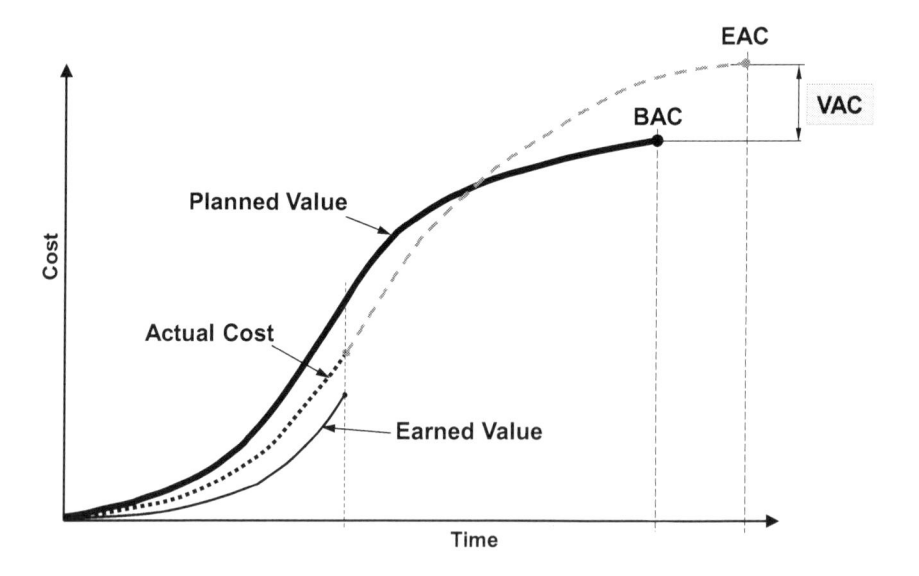

Figure 40: The VAC shows the cost variance at the project end

TCPI – To Complete Performance Index

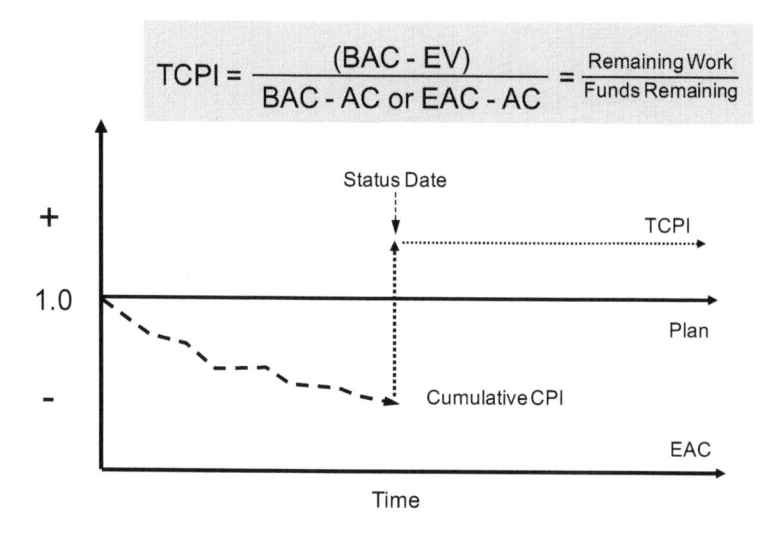

The "To Complete (the remaining Work) Performance Index" describes the necessary cost performance figure to complete the remaining work with the predefined total budget.

With the TCPI, the senior management can see how big the performance figure would have to be to complete the project within budget. The value of the TCPI varies, depending on which project end cost is used as a base. The following project costs are possible:

- the original budget $TCPI_{BAC}$
- the calculated project end costs with different $TCPI_{EAC}$ methods
- a cost ceiling of an order with a fixed price
- any other defined value

The two main formulas for the TCPI are as follows:

$$TCPI_{BAC} = (BAC-EV) / (BAC-AC)$$

$$TCPI_{EAC} = (BAC-EV) / (EAC-AC)$$

A TCPI <1 means that more money than necessary is available for the remaining work. This dream situation usually occurs at a $TCPI_{EAC}$.

A TCPI >1 means that not enough money is available for the remaining work. This challenging situation often occurs at a $TCPI_{BAC}$. This means that ways have to be found in order to save money, so that the (original) budget can be achieved.

$$TCPI = \frac{(BAC - EV)}{BAC - AC \text{ or } EAC - AC} = \frac{\text{Remaining Work}}{\text{Funds Remaining}}$$

Figure 41: To Complete (the remaining Work) Performance Index

ETC – Estimate to Complete

The ETC makes a forecast about the remaining project costs until the end of the project. However, the ETC is only second choice if you want to know how much more costs will occur during the project. The remaining project costs will normally not be calculated, but the project manager makes a detailed estimate using the "Bottom-up" principle on the basis of the revised project plan. Among other things, one has to pay attention to working hours, material costs, overhead costs and risks. The estimate can then be checked with the following formulas.

Similar to the EAC, one can calculate using three methods during the ETC, an optimistic, a realistic and a pessimistic:

$$ETC = (BAC-EV)/1.0 \quad \text{(optimistic Method)}$$

$$ETC_{CPI} = (BAC-EV)/CPI \quad \text{(realistic Method)}$$

$$ETC_{CPIxSPI} = (BAC-EV)/CPIxSPI \quad \text{(pessimistic Method)}$$

If you compare the formulas of the ETC with those of the EAC, then you will find that in ETC simply the adding of the Actual Cost is omitted. Otherwise, the formulas are identical.

The "optimistic method" assumes that the remaining work will be completed within the planned budget. The "realistic method" assumes that the current cost efficiency for the remaining work stays the same - which usually is not the case. The "pessimistic method" calculates the worst-case.

These formulas only provide a statistical forecast and should only be used as a rough comparison sample or as a "second opinion." However, the practice shows that the formula based on the CPI tends to generate more optimistic forecasts. Therefore, one should be cautious. The detailed bottom-up estimate of the remaining work is the alternative method. But it needs quite some time. However, if this estimate is below the ETC_{CPI}, I recommend you to be cautious.

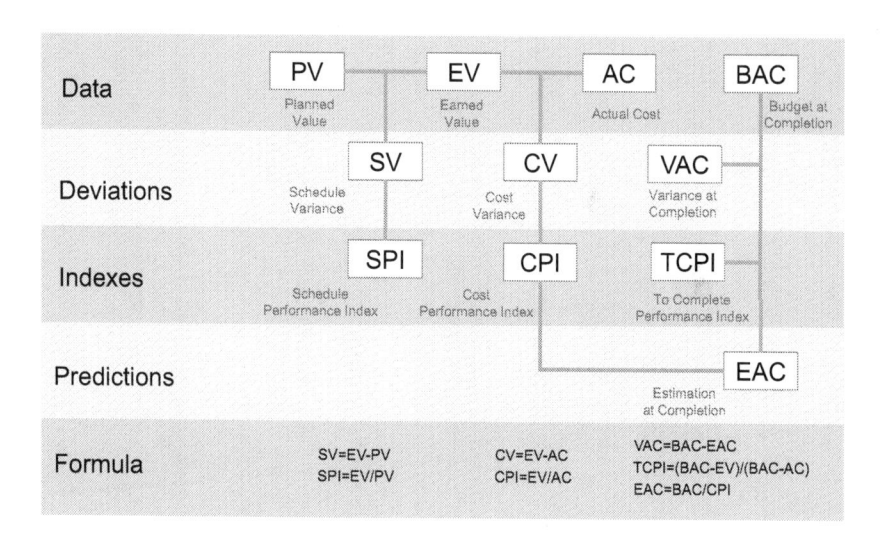

Relations Between the EVM-Performance Figures

All EVM Performance Figures are calculated using one or more of the following four basic data: Planned Value, Earned Value, Actual Cost and Budget at Completion. The following figure shows the relations between EVM Performance Figures and the corresponding formulas on the lowest line very well.

Does your project have cost or schedule problems, or both? The individual EVM Performance Figures will give you a good answer to this question. You obtain an interesting statement about the health status of your project, if you evaluate your project simultaneously according to SV, SPI, CV and CPI. In the following graph, you can see very quickly whether the project has only cost problems, only schedule problems, or if both apply. The bold framed area is the area in which the project should be in the ideal case. However, this condition does not occur very often.

Data	PV Planned Value	EV Earned Value	AC Actual Cost	BAC Budget at Completion
Deviations		SV Schedule Variance	CV Cost Variance	VAC Variance at Completion
Indexes		SPI Schedule Performance Index	CPI Cost Performance Index	TCPI To Complete Performance Index
Predictions				EAC Estimation at Completion
Formula		SV=EV-PV SPI=EV/PV	CV=EV-AC CPI=EV/AC	VAC=BAC-EAC TCPI=(BAC-EV)/(BAC-AC) EAC=BAC/CPI

Figure 42: Relations between the EVM-Performance Figures

Project Forecasts

The colored boxes in the next figure have the following meaning:

- G = Green, Project performs better than planned
- W= White, Project performs according to the plan
- Y= Yellow, Project has cost or schedule problems
- R= Red, Project has cost and schedule problems

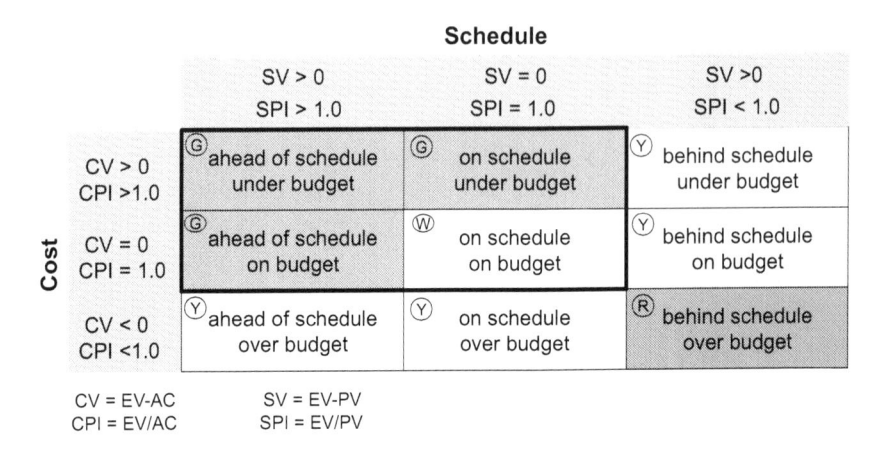

	Schedule		
Cost	SV > 0 SPI > 1.0	SV = 0 SPI = 1.0	SV > 0 SPI < 1.0
CV > 0 CPI > 1.0	(G) ahead of schedule under budget	(G) on schedule under budget	(Y) behind schedule under budget
CV = 0 CPI = 1.0	(G) ahead of schedule on budget	(W) on schedule on budget	(Y) behind schedule on budget
CV < 0 CPI < 1.0	(Y) ahead of schedule over budget	(Y) on schedule over budget	(R) behind schedule over budget

CV = EV-AC   SV = EV-PV
CPI = EV/AC   SPI = EV/PV

Figure 43: Interpretation of basic EVM Performance Figures

EVM and Risk Management Generate Synergies

Risk Management is an ideal complement to EVM. The combined application of EVM and risk management generates synergies, i.e., a greater benefit is generated as if both techniques would be used independently of each other. Herein, the weaknesses of the two methods that are a danger to good decision making will be largely reduced.

The weaknesses of the two methods are represented as follows: EVM-skeptics claim that it was not serious to simply extrapolate the work performed in the past with the calculated performance figures, such as SPI and CPI, into the future, thus making forecasts of the final project costs or of the project end date. However, the future does not act like the past. Exactly at this point, EVM begins. Once you know the calculated – and usually unpleasant - forecasts, you will take actions to ensure that the calculated forecasts do not occur. Despite the actions taken, it is not possible for you to drive a car just looking into the rearview mirror. The risk would be too big. You also need to look forward to help you discover potential obstacles on the way. This is exactly what you do with risk management in your project.

"The best way to predict the future is to learn from the past."

Risk Management looks into the future. It acts like a forward-looking radar, searching in the uncertain and unclear future for dangers which should be avoided. However, the radar is not only looking for dangers, but also for opportunities that could generate additional profits. The sole orientation towards the future is a great strength of risk management, but at the same time a weakness too. Things that happened before today's date, are little or not at all important to risk management. The way the project has reached the present position is not relevant to the risk management process either. Although risk management looks towards the future, it does not completely ignore the past. The "lessons learned" from other, earlier projects help make risk management even more effective.

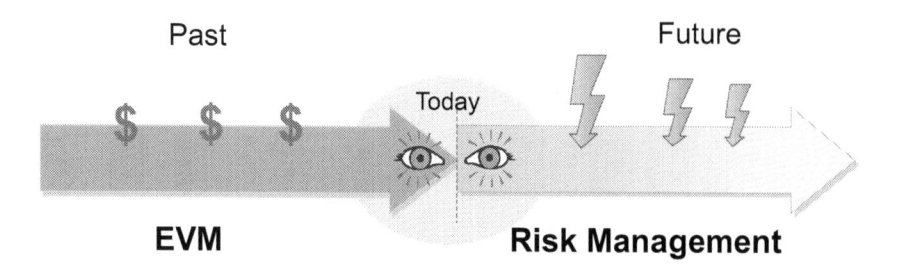

Figure 44: EVM and Risk Management generate Synergies

Project Forecasts

The combination of EVM and risk management brings great synergies in finding potential problems in projects in the constellation of past and future orientation, because they complement each other very well and at the same time, they compensate each other's weaknesses.

Earned Value Management Reporting

The Reporting Dilemma

There is an old accounting saying that even Peter Drucker quotes, "If you can't measure it, you can't manage it." We have taken this in the business world to heart and therefore, a lot of paper is generated, which should reveal us the truth. This information in the project environment includes: project reports, milestone reports, budget reports, risk reports, forecasts, etc. It is understandable that for many project managers project reporting is considered annoying, meaningless and tedious work with no added value for the project. This is then directly reflected in the relevance, the quality and timely submission of the status report.

The 2003 version of the Chaos Report by the Standish Group acknowledges that only 34 percent of all IT-projects can be declared as successful. Do we still not have enough metrics or do we use the wrong ones? Many project managers spend up to 30% of their working time on project reports and the creation of beautiful presentations for the senior management. The benefit that these reports provide is often very low. Why is that? Is the motivation of the project manager or project team members to blame for this dilemma, or is it because of insufficient training?

A big problem is that many of these project reports and presentations have no real significance on the true progress of the project, on deviations as well as problems and risks. The real health of the project remains mostly hidden.

Earned Value Management Reporting

Reasons for the poor quality of reporting are:

- No meaningful performance figures
- Too comprehensive, time-consuming reports
- The reports are not user-friendly (not suitable for the senior management)
- The periodicity of the reports are not adapted to the project type or project duration
- Lack of motivation of the project managers and project team members
- Insufficient or no software tools for project reporting

Another issue that doesn't make the situation any easier is that the reporting is always influenced by the subjective assessment of the project manager. The subjectivity is evident through the perspective of the project manager in his assessment and what then is written effectively in the project report. The project manager writes in the project report what he wants to say - what he doesn't want to say won't be in it. It even happens that the project sponsor stipulates what should not be mentioned before the report is handed on to the project portfolio manager, to the steering committee or to the senior management.

We should be honest. Do those reports really show the senior management how the project has developed, how it probably will evolve and how it will end? I don't think so.

Status Reporting With Added Value

A meaningful and honest status reporting is one of the best ways to get support for the project. But it can also mean the fast end of the project, which could be a benefit for the company – but this does not necessarily comply with the desires of the project manager.

What features should a status report have? It should be short and accurate and only contain relevant information. In order for senior management to understand the project status report which is based on EVM data, it should receive a basic training during EVM implementation. This way, it can understand the components of the status report and the importance of the performance figures. Earned Value Management should therefore be integrated into all discussions of the project status.

The following points should be noted when reporting status with EVM performance figures:

- The environment/culture in the company should be mature enough so that the correspondent should not get punished by bad news: "Don't shoot the messenger."
- Provide all involved people with the appropriate training so that definitions and requirements can be understood.
- Clearly define the data, which should be monitored and reported.
- Define clear rules of how often, to whom and to what extent it should be reported.
- Define the reporting periods, according to the duration and risk of the project.
- The early warning system should also show changes in trend and risks.
- Conduct regular project status meetings, where project performance, monitoring of corrective measures, as well as risks and problems are discussed.
- Show integrity – even if a lot is going poorly, you should provide the senior management with corresponding information.
- As recipient of status reports, you should not always believe in all reported data. Do plausibility checks whenever something appears "strange" or when your gut tells you otherwise.

How to Collect Data in EVM

Collecting and reporting data with or without EVM is perceived by many project managers and project team members as annoying work without added value for the project. In order to be successful, each project performance measurement system must be accepted by all project team members and project managers. Since Earned Value Management provides a deeper insight into project work, it could be perceived by some employees or suppliers as their evaluation. Therefore, it is important that the measuring system should not be considered as an evaluation of the individual but of the project and should be communicated as such.

How to Collect the Most Important Project Data

If project data is collected and reported quickly and easily by the project team, then this contributes significantly to the acceptance of the reporting. Senior management will be more effective when it can focus on a few, but meaningful, critical values, such as important performance figures, risks, problems and changes. More documents and administration would be a nightmare for the project manager and the project team. Therefore, it is very important that the additional effort remains low and only necessary information should be collected.

The data collection should be a by-product of the existing reporting. Thus, the effort is not considered as an additional burden. The quality of the collected data should only be as detailed and accurate as necessary, not just to the decimal point. The ultimate goal would be that all data in its development, e.g., at the project team member, are entered into a centralized project information system.

The most important steps to a good data collection are:

- Determining an appropriate work package size
- Defining how project progress is determined
- Defining how project costs are determined
- Focusing only on the important, critical values

If work packages are too small, then an excessive amount of work and a red tape is the result for the project team when reporting. If work packages are too big, then there is a great danger that the work progress is no longer measured periodically and control measures are taken too late. If the work progress is reported monthly, then the work package duration should be shorter than one month, so about two to three weeks.

The project data should be evaluated not later than five days after the end of the month, in order to be used as an early warning system. In short and/or complex, risky projects, it is even useful to make weekly evaluations of the EVM data. Only this way, one can react quickly and measures take effect faster. However, this state is a pipe dream for many companies.

In practice the whole reporting process is often too slow because many steps are processed manually and integrated software support is lacking. With the current Enterprise Project Management Software Systems and the efficient collection of project data from the producer, an effective reporting is substantially supported.

Reporting With EVM – Same Amount of Effort, Better Quality!

EVM has the reputation of being a lot of effort in data collection and reporting of the data. This is far from being true! It is the same data that you need during the normal reporting – the evaluation is done by the software. The interpreting of the data, the defining and communicating of actions are the same as in any other reporting. The crucial difference is the high quality of performance figures that are provided by the software. From these, effective actions and decisions can be derived.

This data must be collected from each work package, which is in progress:

- Planned Value
- Actual Cost
- Work progress (according to the defined Earned Value Method)

You will be surprised that there is not more information to collect than in normal reporting. Herein, the Actual Cost rather only plays a subordinate role. To calculate the Earned Value, you only need the Planned Value and work progress; however, the Actual Cost is not necessary for this. The Schedule Variance and the SPI can be determined without knowing the Actual Cost. For the calculation of the Cost Variance, you only require the summed Actual Cost of all work packages to the status date. The cost of collecting the data remains low when there are reliable, automatic interfaces between the used project management software and the corporate financial system (e.g., SAP FI/CO).

How to Determine Work Progress and Actual Cost

You can determine work progress of work packages easier by defining small and short work packages from the beginning forward. Then, you can probably use the 0/100 EV Method for most work packages. This way you achieve that the work packages are completed within a reporting period, or even better, between two status meetings. When summarizing the data of the work packages to the Control Account, the inaccuracies of the 0/100 EV-method will offset one another. At project start, when only a few work packages are in progress, the summed data is still relatively imprecise; however, the longer the project takes, the more accurate are the calculated data of the Earned Value and the corresponding performance figures.

Again, we return briefly to the Actual Cost. This is usually the most important data base for all the traditional controlling activities. Unfortunately, these are often obtained with quite some time delay from the accounting and then generally with an incorrect time allocation, as the entry date often does not match the date of the incurred costs. In double-entry accounting, the invoice receipt date is valid as the date on which costs incurred. However, from a project perspective, the date of performance provision is valid.

Earned Value Management Reporting

EVM-System – Inputs and Outputs

In the following figure, you can see what data is required for the Earned Value Management System in order to generate appropriate management information. As a basis for comparison, planned data of the project is required for further processing. During project execution, the system obtains the actual data and the data of project progress according to the chosen EV Method. From these data, the EVM System calculates the corresponding EVM Performance Figures and forecast values, which are used for reporting to the senior management. If necessary, the senior management decides on corrective actions that bring the project back on track.

If one of the input values is not complete or of poor quality, then this causes an impairment of the Earned Value Management System. This results in the fact that the calculated results probably do not show the real state of the project and that the calculated forecasts are wrong, too.

"The results are not better than the input!"

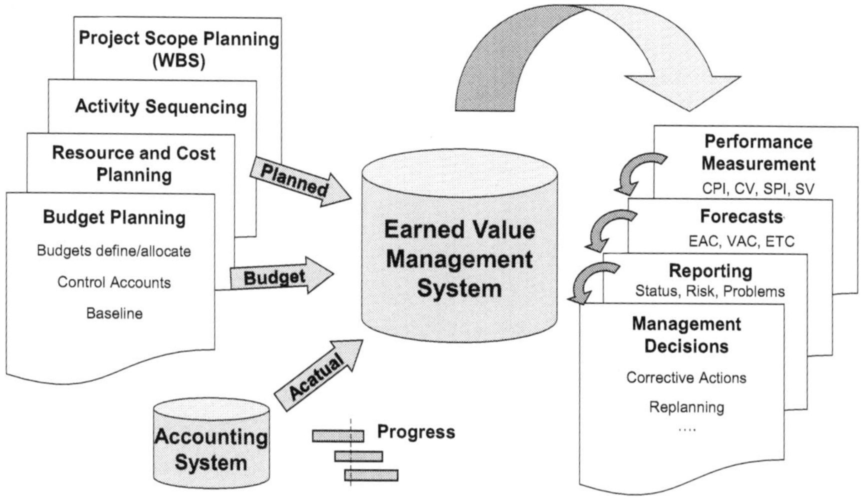

Figure 45: The Inputs and Outputs of the EVM System

Data and Variance Analysis

The easiest work in EVM is probably the data analysis, because it is done by software. Within a fraction of a second, you can see the result in many performance figures and graphs. Now it is getting interesting. How is the project doing?

Immediately, the focus is on the negative performance figures, as well as the downwards pointing CPI Trend curves. Whenever storm clouds appear and nothing works out as planned, get to the root causes of the problem! Now it is important that you ask a lot of questions – to yourself and to the project team. The first two questions are:

- Are there new deviations?
- Did the existing deviations become larger or smaller?

Most of the time, there are no immediate answers to these two questions. However, the following four auxiliaries can help:

- Trend analysis – Where were we – where are we today?
- Projection into the future – Are the performance figures getting better or worse?
- Focus on problems – What are the significant drivers?
- Variance analysis – What do we do about it?

Go in Variance Analysis to the Root

If deviations are present, it is often not so easy to immediately find the causes for them because the calculated performance figures apply to the whole Control Account. This usually consists of several work packages. Now, you need to go deeper and find out in which work package problems are present. When you find the work package in question, it is crucial to analyze the problem and to define actions in order to resolve the problems and/or subsequent problems.

Before EVM data are published with the status report, it is good practice to discuss them first within the project team. This way, the control account manager or work package manager can explain any discrepancies or, if necessary, e.g., if it was not correctly reported, corrections can be made in the data.

In the problem analysis and definition of actions, you should ask yourself these questions:

- What is the problem and how did it occur?
- What are the impacts on time, cost, quality and performance?
- What are the impacts on the other work packages?
- What corrective actions are already planned or taken?
- What are the expected results of the corrective actions?

These Questions Help You Make the Decision:

The project is behind schedule:

- Is the project time critical? Are there contractual penalties?
- Can we permit to work overtime?
- Can we execute work in parallel?
- Are there any technical innovations that could speed up the process?
- Is it useful to carry out a planning assessment to point to impacts, such as the project or program?

The project is over budget:

- Can we work more efficiently, e.g., without interruptions?
- Are there cheaper materials, suppliers or manufacturing methods?
- Can certain jobs be avoided?
- Do we do "gold plating" instead of only meeting the requirements?
- Are costs incorrectly entered? Can some costs be charged on other projects or organizations?

Even if you have chosen the work package size correctly, likely all actions are too late because the work package took less than one reporting period and has just been finished. Therefore, the damage has already occurred – there is nothing left to save. Now you should examine the consequences of this problem, e.g., delays, and the impact of the problem on the following work packages. This is especially important when work packages are affected on the critical path of the project schedule. At the same time, you learn your lessons through this case, so that such problems can be avoided in the future.

There is a simple action to be closer to all events and to combat problems faster: weekly project status meetings in which project status, problems and risks are focused on. Weekly project meetings are very valuable activities to prevent bad surprises. Another action would be weekly EVM evaluations, of which you learn more on page 122.

The Meaningful Status Report

In order to help the senior management find a decision quickly, the status report has to provide objective and reliable statements on project status, represent forecasts, risks and problems and be immediately available.

The project status report does not have to be a great work, but should rather be short and meaningful as possible. The reason for this is simple: the shorter and more relevant the report, the more likely it is to be read, the faster the feedback and the sooner it is possible to initiate appropriate actions. In this case, only the relevant EVM Performance Figures should be presented in the report. Problems, as well as their impacts and corrective actions, should be presented clearly, so that the management has a base to make decisions. The graphics should be self-explanatory with some previous knowledge and quickly readable, i.e., in less than 5 seconds.

A project status report should have the following properties:

- up to date, short and meaningful
- quickly understandable and not open to interpretation
- represent trends and forecasts
- describe risks, problems, causes and actions

Represent Deviations Clearly

If the status report has the qualities described above, the assessment of the project status is easy and the deviations from the planned status can be quickly understood by senior management.

If deviations are within the defined limits, no actions are necessary. At larger deviations, actions must be described in the status report. In severe cases, this can even result in a replanning of the project, in the reduction of project scope or in the adjustment of project objectives.

The evaluation methods of the status reports provide the following information:

- Trend analysis: Where have we been, where are we now?
- Projection of the future: Will the performance figures become better or worse?
- Focus on problems: What are the significant drivers and possible damages?
- Variance analysis: What do we do about it?

For a fast evaluation, a good project status report should contain a short descriptive part and a graphical part. Herein, arrow or traffic light icons provide a quick overview of the status of the project.

Trust is Good – Observation, Analysis and Asking is Better!

You never know what you can learn from listening. Do you listen to the project team and feel the pulse - or do you just focus on data? If the EVM data only shows minor deviations, but the team speaks about failed tests, technical challenges and weekend work, then you should prick up your ears!

EVM is an important tool in project monitoring, but not the only one. Listen carefully during meetings, ask necessary questions, meet not only with the project team, but also with individual project team members. This will provide you with additional information about the health of the project.

If you, as a member of the senior management, a program manager, project controller or member of the steering committee, receive a status report, you can principally believe in what it says. However, you should be critical and listen to your gut feeling if something appears strange. Ask why something is "that way." Ask follow-up questions and if necessary, go into depth in order to understand certain points better or to analyze. Also, you are responsible for the project. Assume it seriously!

Possible potential problem indicators are:

- Non-meaningful, non-specific descriptions
- Not addressing specific subjects
- Downplaying or not mentioning of risks or problems
- Representing only a short period of time (salami-slicing). No forecasts for the whole project

- Usage of management reserve
- Changes in the Performance Measurement Baseline
- Zero variances over a longer period of time. Everything always looks fine.
- Significant schedule variance. It shows that additional costs will follow later
- Monthly trends go into negative
- Unrealistic or changing EAC

EVM Graphs Bring More Transparency

Graphs say more than a thousand words. This wisdom has long been known. When you represent project costs and EVM Performance Figures graphically, the viewer should have an overview within 5 seconds of how the project is doing. With EVM graphs, you can see very quickly whether the project is healthy, or it urgently needs help. The line graph in the following figure with Planned Value, Earned Value and Actual Cost is often used for this. This graph provides a quick overview of the project status.

In the graph below, you can see different scenarios that may occur in your project. Scenario 4 would actually be desirable, but doesn't usually occur.

- Scenario 1: behind schedule, over budget (Worst Case)
- Scenario 2: behind schedule, under budget
- Scenario 3: ahead of schedule, over budget
- Scenario 4: ahead of schedule, under budget (Best Case)

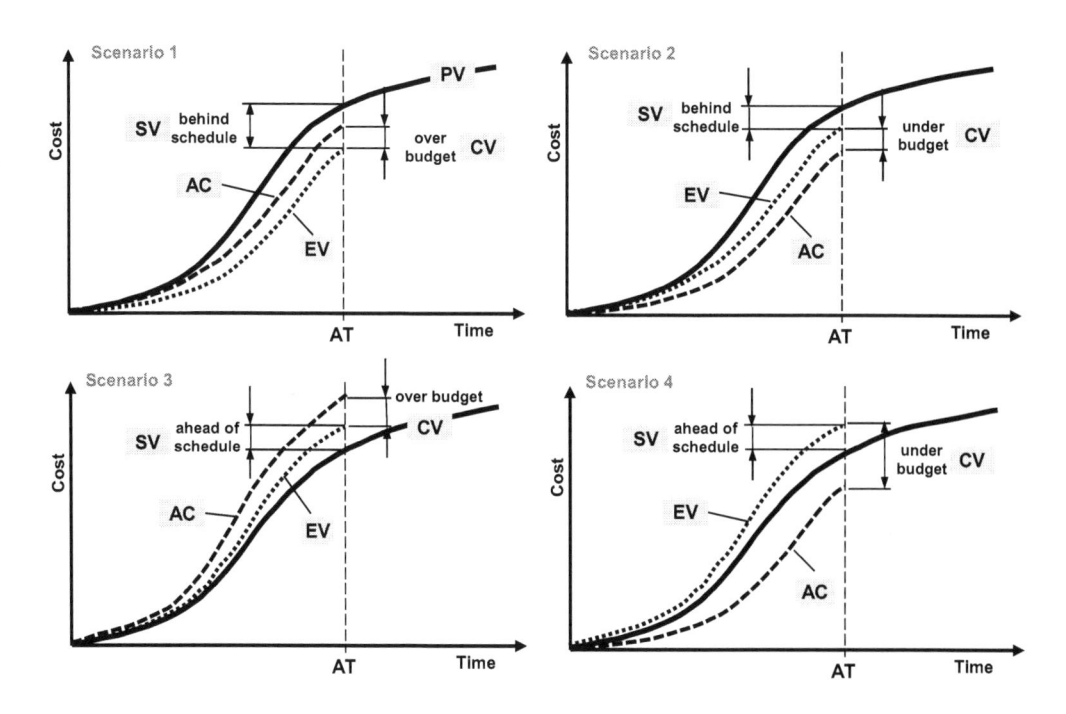

Figure 46: EVM-Graphs with EV, AC and PV

Figure 46 provides a good overview of the costs trend and project progress. However, I prefer graphs that show the CPI and SPI. These graphs show the trends more directly and from the beginning of the project. Also changes in trends after actions taken are visible more quickly. Below you will find the four possible scenarios, but this time with SPI and CPI.

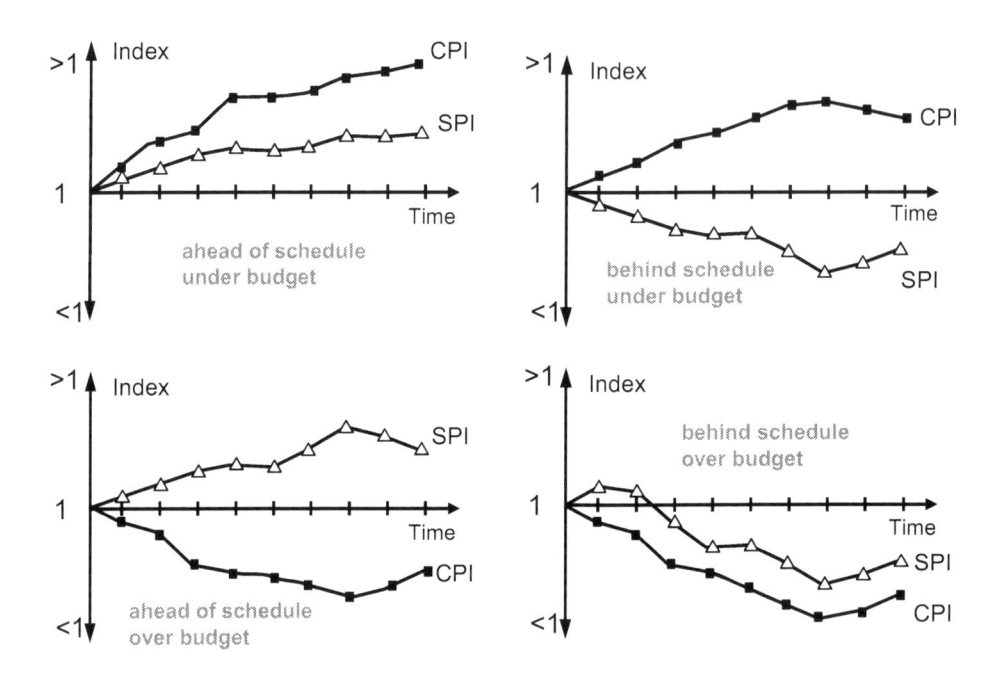

Figure 47: Scenarios with CPI and SPI

EVM-Reporting in Contracts of the U.S. Government

It is not unlikely that you will have to deal with orders of the U.S. government or its major sub-contractors, like Boeing, British Aerospace and Lockheed Martin. In these institutions, however, from a certain project size certain reporting requirements regarding EVM must be met. Previously, the Cost/Schedule Status Report (C/SSR) was used for smaller projects – nowadays only the Cost Performance Report (CPR) is used. You can find a general overview of the reporting requirements in the following figure.

Where	Commercial or Defense			US Department of Defense (DoD) *		
	Small Companies	Larger Companies			
When	As required	Corporate policy, "enterprise wide"	Contracts (>12 months) <$20M	Contracts (>12 months) ≥$20M but <$50M Not required: firm- fixed price contracts	Contracts (>12 months) ≥$50M Not required: firm- fixed price contracts
Reports	Streamlined, simple	Tailored to needs	CPR Form 1 and 5 incl. Cost-benefit analysis	CPR Form 1 and 5 Integratet Master Schedule	CPR all Formats Integratet Master Schedule
Method	Core EV principles	Tailored applications	ANSI/EIA-748 compliance should be tailored based on risk	ANSI/EIA-748 compliant	ANSI/EIA-748 compliant and validated

* DoD EVM Implementation Guide April 2005

Figure 48: Reporting requirements of the Department of Defense

The Cost Performance Report (CPR) is a comprehensive monthly EVM report, which consists of five different formats:

- Format 1: Work Breakdown Structure (WBS) - Budgets and EVM Performance Figures for each WBS element
- Format 2: Organizational Categories - Budget and EVM Performance Figures are broken down into operating organizational units
- Format 3: Baseline - Forecast of monthly changes in the Baseline, Management Reserve and Undistributed Budget
- Format 4: Staffing (Manpower) - Current hours and forecasts of the to be performed hours per month per organizational unit
- Format 5: Variance Analysis Report - Variance analysis with EVM Performance Figures and description of each WBS element

For all projects < $50 million, Format 1 (WBS) and Format 5 are applied (Variance Analysis Report). Many customers outside the government departments keep it similar. From my point of view, Format 5 is the most important one. It contains all relevant EVM Performance Figures and describes the analysis of the problem with impacts and corresponding actions per WBS element in a text form.

All performance measurement data, which are reported in the CPR, are derived from a formal Earned Value Management System (EVMS). Herein, software systems, such as "Deltek wInsight Analytics," are great help for the evaluation, since they master the corresponding DoD-formats. All changes in the project baseline, Management Reserve (MR) and Contingency Reserve (CR) should be comprehensible through EVM and the CPR.

When Shorter Reporting Cycles Are Meaningful

In the past, cost reporting with time cards, Word or Excel forms was still very cumbersome. The transfer of this data to other systems and its evaluation was extremely time consuming. Today, where highly developed project management software and ERP-systems are used in many businesses, reporting (e.g., of work effort) is done quickly and easily. If each project team member enters his working hours in the evening before leaving the company, one always has the current data in the system. Under these conditions, one could virtually look at the screen in real-time and would know how the project is doing. So why do most projects still report monthly? You will get the following answers to this question: "That is far too much effort; it has always been this way; we do not know anything else; our processes are not suitable for shorter periods; in our company, projects are not that important; we do not benefit from that." Yes, these answers are more or less the facts.

In which projects are shorter reporting periods meaningful?

- Generally: Expensive projects with a duration of less than one year
- Complex, risky, expensive projects
- Projects with "fixed" end date and high contract penalties
- Projects that imply a major financial risk for the company

And what benefit does this all have?

- The weekly evaluation shortens the cycle for the identification of the problem, the definition of corrective actions as well as for the solution of the problem and its verification.
- It enables the management to take corrective action at the earliest possible time.
- The early focus reduces risks and surprises significantly.

The "Joint Strike Fighter" F-35 Program (combat aircraft) of the DoD, which costs about $ 388 billion and takes more than 12 years to develop, involves Lockheed Martin, Northrop Grumman and BAE SYSTEMS as its major subcontractors. The EVM-project data (only direct people effort) of all project participants (including subcontractors) is reported weekly and then evaluated centrally. In the weekly report, only the deviations in people effort, performance figures and trends are evaluated; the monthly status report is more comprehensive. Other billion-dollar military projects with thousands of work packages keep it similar.

According to the statements of the F-35 project manager, the biggest challenge in the weekly reporting and evaluation was changing the management culture. "The challenge in weekly EVM reporting does not cost anything – but it pays off!" When will you accept the challenge? A reporting cycle of 2 weeks would already be a step forward.

Some important requirements for a weekly EVM-reporting are:

- High project management maturity in the company
- Appropriate project management software or a combination of software products
- Automated processes
- A higher instance that demands for a weekly transparency
- A well trained team

It is crucial that you keep your reporting as easy as possible, focusing on a timely manner instead of reporting comprehensively. It is better to provide senior management with less information, but as close as possible to real-time, so that it can make good and quick decisions, rather than beautiful, comprehensive reports that nobody reads and that are delivered too late to generate benefits.

Earned Value Management Reporting

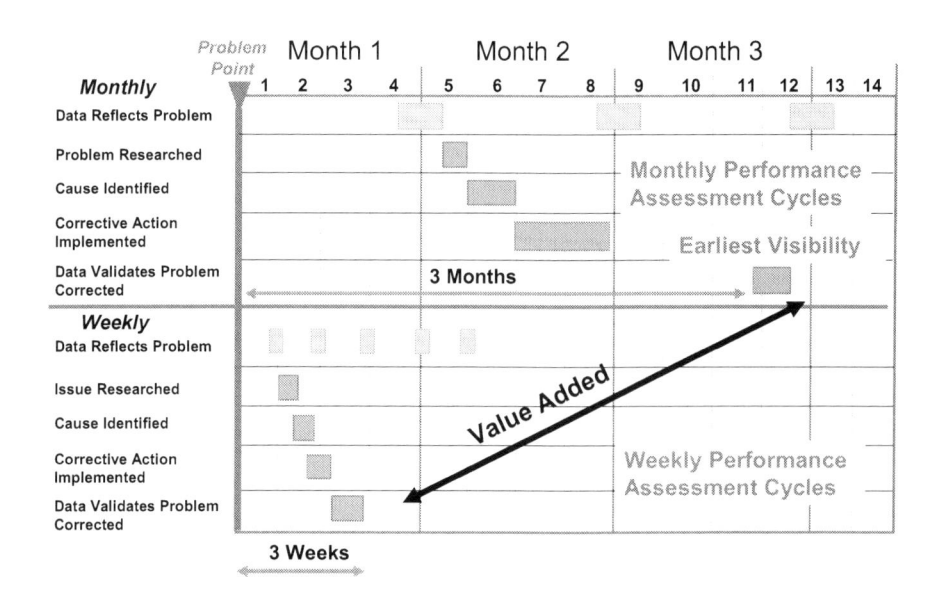

Figure 49: Weekly EVM-Reporting discovers problems earlier

Simple EVM On All Your Projects!

The Earned Value Management Concept must be good, because it has existed for 40 years. Do you know management concepts that have survived such a long time and have been applied constantly? There are probably only a few. However, the comprehensive 35 C/SCSC-criteria of 1965 and the 32 EVMS criteria according to ANSI/EIA-748 that have arisen in 1996, have a drawback - they were written for large, complex programs and projects. For the development of combat aircraft or nuclear power plants, they are ideal and suitable - but for the majority of projects, they are too comprehensive. The essential elements of the 32 EVMS-criteria can be summarized in 10 fundamental requirements[5] that can be used in all projects. If you apply these 10 points, then you have already met the most important of the 32 EVMS-criteria with relatively little effort and practiced very good EVM. For each point, you will find a reference to the ANSI/EIA criteria.

The 10 most important points for a simple and good EVM

1. **Define the complete project scope.** You have to define 100% of the project scope in the WBS. Define all work, deliverables and milestones. This is the basis for all further activities for point 2 to 10. (EVM Criterion 1)

2. **Determine who will perform the defined work including the identification of all critical procurements.** Do you have the know-how and experienced workers internally or do you have to procure it? Contracts with foreign suppliers contain considerable risks and make the project more complex. Also, subcontractors must be included in the EVM concept. Procured components receive their own work packages separated by internal staff effort. (EVM Criterion 2)

3. **Plan and schedule the defined work.** The schedule reflects the authorized scope and timeframe and the basis for the baseline. Define dependencies between work packages and determine and manage the critical path of the project. (EVM Criterion 6)

4. **Estimate the required resources and formally authorize budgets.** Each WBS element requires resources and the appropriate budget to get the job done. The management assesses the required resources and approves a value in the form of an authorized budget. WBS elements never contain contingencies or Management Reserves. (EVM Criterion 9)

---

[5] Quentin W. Fleming and Joel M. Koppelman – Start with "simple" Earned Value on all your Projects, June 2006 – Crosstalk; The Journal of Defence Software Engineering

5. **Determine the metrics to define the Earned Value.** Define for each work package and planned work measurable and verifiable criteria to measure the accomplishment of Planned Value into Earned Value. These may be specific, weighted milestones within work packages or tasks with defined values. (EVM Criterion 7)

6. **Establish a performance measurement baseline that adds up all Control Account Plans (CAPs).** Define CAPs that are to be monitored with EVM. CAPs include specific work packages or subprojects, which as a whole adds up the in the resulting time-based project baseline. (EVM Criterion 8)

7. **Record all direct costs consistently from your financial accounting system, in accordance with the defined budgets and control account.** Record all of the direct costs of monitored control accounts in timely intervals and put them in relation to the authorized budgets. (EVM criterion 16)

8. **Continuously monitor Earned Value performance to determine cost and schedule deviations from the baseline plan.** Monitor cost and schedule results against the authorized baseline and calculate on control account level at least CPI and SPI as well as CV and SV. Each behind-schedule task should be assessed to its criticality, especially if it's on the critical path or carries a high risk to the project. (EVM Criterion 22)

9. **Use EVM performance figures to forecast the final project cost and for management reports.**
Determine the EAC and the estimated cost at the end of the project. At least monthly, report significant deviations, their causes and actions to the management to control of the program. (EVM criterion 27)

10. **Manage the authorized scope by approving or rejecting all changes, and incorporating approved changes in a timely manner.** The Performance Measurement Baseline is only as good as the management of project changes. Any change has to go through a controlled process and after approval needs to be incorporated quickly into project planning. (EVM criterion 28)

The Earned Value Management System Criteria

From C/SCSC to ANSI

By the year 1997, the DoD defined the requirements for an Earned Value Management System (EVMS). Companies from the private industry who wanted to get an order from the DoD, had to apply an EVMS, that met these requirements. These were defined as 35 criteria (thirty-five Cost/Schedule Control Systems Criteria (C / SCSC)). Other agencies of the U.S. government and some other governments, such as Australia, New Zealand, Canada and Sweden, took over identical or similar criteria.

In 1995, a committee of the National Defense Industrial Association (NDIA) started to revise the 35 criteria. The result was a so-called "industrial-version," which was called "Earned Value Management System (EVMS) Criteria". This contained 32 criteria that is three less than the original C/SCSC. In December 1996, these revised criteria were accepted by the Under Secretary of Defense for Acquisition & Technology and in 1997 the next update was added to the DoD Manual 5000.2R. At the same time, a shift from the U.S. government to private industry took place as the "owner" of EVMS.

In 1998, the American National Standards Institute/Electronic Industries Association (ANSI/EIA) declared the EVMS criteria as a national standard. The result was the ANSI/EIA-748 standard, which in turn was also adopted by the DoD. Private industry has now found more access to EVM, not because it was required by the government, but because it was a so-called "best practice" tool for all project managers in private industry.

In March 2013, the ANSI/EIA-748-B was replaced by ANSI/EIA-748-C. It made only minor amendments and provided more details. For the 32 criteria, however, nothing substantial has changed.

The 32 EVMS Criteria

The ANSI/EIA-748 standard and the EVMS criteria contained therein were deliberately kept very general. Indeed, companies have the flexibility to implement and apply the new management system in accordance with its management style and its business environment. Therefore, the National Defense Industrial Association (NDIA) Program Management Systems Committee (PMSC) published the following document: "NDIA PMSC ANSI/EIA-748-A Standard for Earned Value Management Systems Intent Guide." This "Intent Guide" provides an additional insight into each of the 32 EVMS criteria and describes in detail the intent and the management value of the individual criteria. If you are required to use ANSI/IEA-748, but even if you want to delve deeper with this topic, then you should get this standard and the "Intent Guide". The documents also give good ideas to introduce EVM in your company. Both documents can be downloaded from the Internet as PDF files.

The standard contains, in addition to the 32 EVMS criteria, an overview of the main EVM terminology and process descriptions for the WBS creation, budgeting, scheduling and resource planning, determination of the Earned Value, performance measurement, etc.

The 32 EVMS criteria are divided into the following five groups:

- Organization (of the project): Criteria 1-5
- Planning, Scheduling, & Budgeting: Criteria 6-15
- Accounting Considerations: Criteria 16-21
- Analysis and Management Reports: Criteria 22-27
- Revisions and Data Maintenance: Criteria 28-32

On the following pages you will find the list of the 32 EVMS criteria.

Earned Value Management Reporting

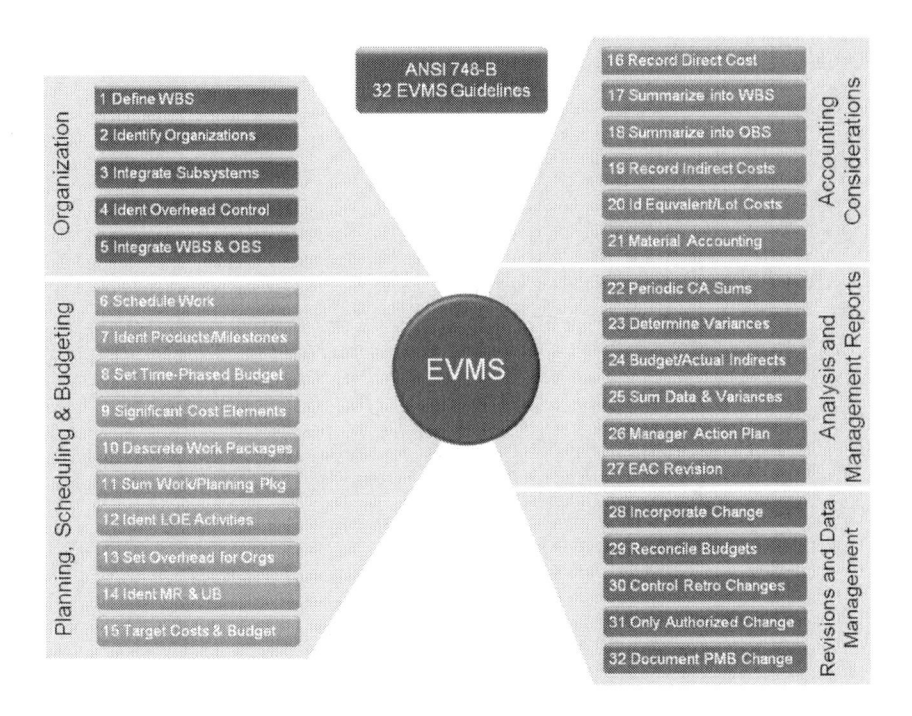

Figure 50: The 32 EVMS criteria at a glance

Organization

1. Define the authorized work elements for the program. A work breakdown structure (WBS), tailored for effective internal management control, is commonly used in this process.

2. Identify the program organizational structure including the major subcontractors responsible for accomplishing the authorized work, and define the organizational elements in which work will be planned and controlled.

3. Provide for the integration of the company's planning, scheduling, budgeting, work authorization and cost accumulation processes with each other, and as appropriate, the program work breakdown structure and the program organizational structure.

4. Identify the company organization or function responsible for controlling overhead (indirect costs).

5. Provide for integration of the program work breakdown structure and the program organizational structure in a manner that permits cost and schedule performance measurement by elements of either or both structures as needed.

Earned Value Management Reporting

Planning and Budgeting

6. Schedule the authorized work in a manner which describes the sequence of work and identifies significant task interdependencies required to meet the requirements of the program.

7. Identify physical products, milestones, technical performance goals, or other indicators that will be used to measure progress.

8. Establish and maintain a time-phased budget baseline, at the control account level, against which program performance can be measured. Budget for far-term efforts may be held in higher-level accounts until an appropriate time for allocation at the control account level. Initial budgets established for performance measurement will be based on either internal management goals or the external customer negotiated target cost including estimates for authorized but undefinitized work. On government contracts, if an over target baseline is used for performance measurement reporting purposes, prior notification must be provided to the customer.

9. Establish budgets for authorized work with identification of significant cost elements (labor, material, etc.) as needed for internal management and for control of subcontractors.

10. To the extent it is practical to identify the authorized work in discrete work packages, establish budgets for this work in terms of dollars, hours, or other measurable units. Where the entire control account is not subdivided into work packages, identify the far term effort in larger planning packages for budget and scheduling purposes.

11. Provide that the sum of all work package budgets plus planning package budgets within a control account equals the control account budget.

12. Identify and control level of effort activity by time-phased budgets established for this purpose. Only that effort which is unmeasurable or for which measurement is impractical may be classified as level of effort.

13. Establish overhead budgets for each significant organizational component of the company for expenses which will become indirect costs. Reflect in the program budgets, at the appropriate level, the amounts in overhead pools that are planned to be allocated to the program as indirect costs.

14. Identify management reserves and undistributed budget.

15. Provide that the program target cost goal is reconciled with the sum of all internal program budgets and management reserves.

Earned Value Management Reporting

Accounting Considerations

16. Record direct costs in a manner consistent with the budgets in a formal system controlled by the general books of account.

17. When a work breakdown structure is used, summarize direct costs from control accounts into the work breakdown structure without allocation of a single control account to two or more work breakdown structure elements.

18. Summarize direct costs from the control accounts into the contractor's organizational elements without allocation of a single control account to two or more organizational elements.

19. Record all indirect costs which will be allocated to the contract.

20. Identify unit costs, equivalent units costs, or lot costs when needed.

21. For EVMS, the material accounting system will provide for:

    (1) Accurate cost accumulation and assignment of costs to control accounts in a manner consistent with the budgets using recognized, acceptable, costing techniques.

    (2) Cost performance measurement at the point in time most suitable for the category of material involved, but no earlier than the time of progress payments or actual receipt of material.

    (3) Full accountability of all material purchased for the program including the residual inventory.

Analysis and Management Reports

22. At least on a monthly basis, generate the following information at the control account and other levels as necessary for management control using actual cost data from, or reconcilable with, the accounting system:

    (1) Comparison of the amount of planned budget and the amount of budget earned for work accomplished. This comparison provides the schedule variance.

    (2) Comparison of the amount of the budget earned the actual (applied where appropriate) direct costs for the same work. This comparison provides the cost variance.

23. Identify, at least monthly, the significant differences between both planned and actual schedule performance and planned and actual cost performance, and provide the reasons for the variances in the detail needed by program management.

24. Identify budgeted and applied (or actual) indirect costs at the level and frequency needed by management for effective control, along with the reasons for any significant variances.
25. Summarize the data elements and associated variances through the program organization and/or work breakdown structure to support management needs and any customer reporting specified in the contract.
26. Implement managerial actions taken as the result of earned value information.
27. Develop revised estimates of cost at completion based on performance to date, commitment values for material, and estimates of future conditions. Compare this information with the performance measurement baseline to identify variances at completion important to company management and any applicable customer reporting requirements including statements of funding requirements.

Revisions and Data Maintenance

28. Incorporate authorized changes in a timely manner, recording the effects of such changes in budgets and schedules. In the directed effort prior to negotiation of a change, base such revisions on the amount estimated and budgeted to the program organizations.
29. Reconcile current budgets to prior budgets in terms of changes to the authorized work and internal replanning in the detail needed by management for effective control.
30. Control retroactive changes to records pertaining to work performed that would change previously reported amounts for actual costs, earned value, or budgets. Adjustments should be made only for correction of errors, routine accounting adjustments, effects of customer or management directed changes, or to improve the baseline integrity and accuracy of performance measurement data.
31. Prevent revisions to the program budget except for authorized changes.
32. Document changes to the performance measurement baseline.

Appendix 12

Earned Value Management Glossar

A

Actual Cost (AC) – The costs actually incurred and recorded in accomplishing the work. Former name was Actual Cost of Work Performed (ACWP).

ACWP - Actual Cost of Work Performed , *see* Actual Cost (AC)

ANSI/EIA-748 – American standard called "Earned Value Management System (EVMS)", which describes the implementation and use of EVM.

Apportioned Effort –Work that is not directly definable and measurable. It is proportionally dependent on the performance and progress of another related activity. The activities of quality assurance is an example for this.

Authorized Unpriced Work (AUW) – The authorized work for which no definite budget has been set. This is typically due to negotiations not being completed on contract changes.

Authorized Work – The work for which authority to proceed has been given; in an Earned Value situation this implies that a budget has been approved for it and it is contained within the project plan.

B

BAC – *see* Budget at Completion (BAC)

Baseline – An agreed plan against which all changes will be recorded and all progress and costs will be measured. *see also* Performance Measurement Baseline (PMB).

Baseline Freeze Date (BFD) – The date when initial baseline planning is completed, and the baseline becomes subject to change control procedures.

Baseline Change Control – The system used to establish, analyze, communicate, and record approved changes to the program baseline.

Appendix

Baseline Review (BR) – A review which is carried out by the customer or sponsor. It checks on a sample basis, whether the contractor has implemented the contractually agreed project monitoring systems and the baseline.

BCWP – Budgeted Cost of Work Performed, *see* Earned Value (EV)

BCWS – Budgeted Cost of Work Scheduled, *see* Planned Value (PV)

Budget – Total resources (measured in dollars, man-hours, or other definitive units) that are formally allocated for the accomplishment of a specific task or group of tasks.

Budget at Completion (BAC) – The total budget established for the completion of the Program, Control Account, Work Package, or task.

Burden – Overhead expenses that are allocated to the appropriate direct staff costs and/or material costs. *see also* Indirect cost

C

C/SCSC – *see* Cost/Schedule Control System Criteria

C/SSR – *see* Cost/Schedule Status Report

CA – *see* Control Account

CAM – *see* Control Account Manager

CAP – *see* Control Account Plan

CBB – *see* Contract Budget Base

CFSR – *see* Contract Funds Status Report

CPI – *see* Cost Performance Index

CPR – *see* Cost Performance Report

CTC – *see* Contract Target Cost

CTP – *see* Contract Target Price

CV – *see* Cost Variance

CWBS – *see* Contract Work Breakdown Structure

Charge Number – The account number for work at the lowest level to which a performing organization charges direct or indirect labor, materials, and other costs.

Contract Budget Base (CBB) – The CBB is the sum of the negotiated contract cost plus the Authorized unpriced Work (AUW). This is equal to the sum of all control account budgets, undistributed budgets, summary Level planning budgets and the management reserve.

Appendix

Contract Data Requirements List (CDRL) – An element of the contract that specifies the data submittal requirements.

Contract Funds Status Report (CFSR) – A DoD financial report that provides funding information necessary to update and forecast contract fund requirements.

Contract Target Cost (CTC) – The negotiated cost for the defined original contract incl. all defined, negotiated changes, however without the estimated cost of all authorized but not yet negotiated costs. The CTC is equal to the value of the BAC plus the management or contingency reserve.

Contract Target Price (CTP) – he negotiated estimated cost (CTC) plus profit or fee.

Contract Work Breakdown Structure (CWBS) – The WBS for a specific Government contract that is product-oriented and developed in accordance with MIL-HDBK-881 (Latest Revision). The CWBS provides for the subdivision of contract work into major elements.

Control Account (CA)– (former cost account) The focal point for planning, monitoring, and controlling tasks. The Control Account represents work within a single WBS element, and it is the responsibility of a single organizational unit.

Control Account Manager (CAM) – Person responsible for the Control Account, which often corresponds to the sub-project leader. He manages the provision of services: resources, technology, schedule and cost aspects of his accounts and reports periodically to the project manager.

Control Account Plan (CAP) – A plan for all of the work and effort to be performed in a control account. Each CAP has a definitive scope of work, schedule and time-phased budget.

Cost Account - An outdated name for a control account.

Cost Performance Index (CPI) – The CPI is the cost-related performance figure in EVM. It is the ratio between Earned Value (EV) and the recorded Actual Cost (AC). A CPI greater than 1 is positive (cost underrun), a CPI less than 1 is negative (cost overrun).

Cost Performance Report (CPR) – A US DoD defined report format for reporting cost and schedule progress data for contracts that require EVMS compliance.

Cost/Schedule Control Systems Criteria (C/SCSC) – 35 standards defined by the American Government which has been used since 1967 for private contractors to ensure that specific types of contracts (reimbursable and incentive type) are managed correctly. The 35 C/SCSC standards were replaced by the 32 "Earned Value Management System Criteria" in December 1996

Cost/Schedule Status Report (C/SSR) – A performance measurement report established to capture information on smaller contracts, primarily in U.S. government contracts

Cost Variance (CV) – Is the difference between the Earned Value (EV), and Actual Cost (AC)D

Direct Costs – Personnel costs, material costs and other direct costs which specific, executed project work can be assigned. Direct costs reflect the indirect costs such as overhead and office costs, which are charged as a flat rate to the project.

Discrete Effort – Expenditure for an activity that creates a specific, measurable end product or result. Discrete effort is an ideal work category in EVM.

E

Earned Value (EV) – Value for the physically or intellectually work performed or performance to the status date, expressed in the budgeted cost. Also known as budgeted cost of work performed (BCWP).

ES – Earned Schedule – Value for the planned time of work physically done so far. Corresponds to the period in which the produced amount of Earned Value would have to be worked out.

Estimate at Completion (EAC) – The EAC calculates the estimated total costs of a work package, group of work packages or the project when the defined scope of work is done. The EAC meets the currently allocated costs plus the estimated cost for the completion of the remaining work.

Estimate at Completion EAC(t) – The EAC(t) calculates the total estimated duration of the project upon completion. The EAC(t) corresponds to the Actual Time plus the estimated duration for the completion of the remaining work.

Estimate to Complete (ETC) – The estimated cost for the completion of the remaining authorized work. The ETC equals the BAC minus EV.

I

IBR – *see* Integrated Baseline Review

Appendix

Indirect Costs – Any costs that cannot be assigned directly to a specific contract, project, product or service, such as Management salaries, insurance, heating, rent, etc..

Integrated Baseline Review (IBR) – Review process for contractors of the DoD which must comply with EVMS requirements. It checks whether planning and budgeting on Control Account level is correctly defined and that a realistic budget is available to complete all planned work.

Integrated Master Schedule (IMS) – Is an overall schedule containing the detailed tasks necessary to ensure successful (DoD) program/contract execution. The IMS is used to verify attainability contract objectives, to evaluate progress toward meeting program objectives.

L

Latest Revised Estimate (LRE) – The most recent estimate of the final cost of a project, or part of a project, based on known work. Note, this term is sometimes used interchangeably with the Estimate At Completion (EAC)

Level of Effort (LOE) – A method of costing work which is time dependent rather that associated with any definitive output, for example, support services such as project management or maintaining the project accounts. Value is accrued according to the elapsed time and resources employed rather than observed progress.

M

Management Reserve (MR) – The MR is a budget of the CBB and serves as security for unidentified risks that could lead to unexpected problems. It is under the control of the client or senior management and is only part of the Performance Measurement Baseline (PMB), if it is effectively distributed.

Master Project Schedule – Project plan at the highest level, which provides an overview of the phases of the project, the main interfaces, key milestones and significant work elements.

O

Organizational Breakdown Structure (OBS) – Hierarchical organization structure of the company or an area of the contractor, which executes the project or specific parts of it.

Over Target Baseline (OTB) – New baseline or "recovery budget" that results from a formal reprogramming of the project when the project objectives with the original budget can no longer be achieved. The OTB exceeds the Contract target cost and is authorized by the client.

P

Performance Measurement Baseline (PMB) – The PMB is the sum of all Summary Level Planning Package (SLPP), Control Accounts (CA) and undistributed budget (UB), exclusive of the Management Reserve (MR). The PMB is the time-phased budget, to which the project is measured with Earned Value management indicators.

Planned Value (PV) – The Planned Value describes at any moment the project, the budgeted cost (effort) of the planned work. Former name was Budgeted Cost of Work Scheduled (BCWS).

Planning Package – Planning packages reflect a segment of future work within a control account, which has not yet been broken down further into detailed work packages. A planning package has a defined budget, an estimated start and end date and a work job description.

R

Replanning – A change in the original plan, to meet the contractually authorized requirements. There are two types of Replanning:

1. Internal Replanning – A change in the original plan, which is within the contractually defined project scope. This to compensate for cost, schedule, or technical problems that have made the original plan unrealistic.

2. External Replanning – Changes desired by the customer in form of a change request, which causes a change in the original plan.

Reprogramming – A comprehensive replanning of the remaining project effort, which is normally completed in a revised Total Allocated Budget that exceeds the defined Contract Budget Base (CBB).

Responsibility Assignment Matrix (RAM) – Representation of the relationship between the WBS elements and the responsible corporate organization, which carries out the relevant work.

Rolling Wave Planning – Is the process of project planning in waves as the project proceeds and later details become clearer.

Appendix

S

Schedule Performance Index (SPI) – The SPI is the ratio between the budgeted cost of work performed (Earned Value) and the budgeted cost of work scheduled (Planned Value)

Schedule Performance Index SPI(t) – The SPI(t) is the time-based variant of the SPI. It is the ratio between the planned time of work performed (Earned Schedule) and the Actual Time (AT) at the reporting date.

Schedule Variance (SV) – The SV is the difference between the Earned Value (EV) and Planned Value (PV) at the reporting date.

Schedule Variance SV(t) – Die SV(t) is the time-based variant of the SV. It is the difference between the planned time of work performed (Earned Schedule) and the Actual Time (AT) at the reporting date..

T

To Complete Performance Index (TCPI) – The TCPI is the necessary cost-performance figure to complete the remaining work within the given total cost.

To Complete Schedule Performance Index TSPI(t) – The TSPI (t) shows the efficiency factor necessary to complete the remaining work in the planned project duration.

Total Allocated Budget (TAB) – The TAB is the summary of all budgets for the creation of contractually, authorized work. The TAB includes the performance measurement baseline plus the management reserve. The TAB must always represent the Contract Budget Base (CBB)..

Technical Performance Measurement (TPM) – TPM is used for monitoring the attainment of the technical degree and the technical risks. It provides early warning signs of deviations from specified requirements, which might end up with some probability in higher costs or scheduling problems.

U

Undistributed Budget (UB) – The UB is a project budget, which was only roughly defined and not clearly associated with a control account or work package. The UB is a temporary budget and should be assigned as early as possible a Control Account and a Work Package.

V

Variance at Completion (VAC) – The VAC is the difference between the budget at completion (BAC) and the Estimate at Completion (EAC). A negative result indicates that the project must expect a budget overrun at the end of the project.

W

Work Authorization Document (WAD) – The WAD authorizes and documents the responsibilities and competencies within the specified time schedule, budget and the specifications for all individuals or organizations that work on the project.

Work Breakdown Structure (WBS) – The WBS shows the full hierarchical arrangement of all deliverables and all major activities that must be performed by the project. The WBS can be designed product, phase, or mixed-oriented and contains at the lowest level the work packages. It is hierarchically so deep, respectively detailed structured so that the project can be effectively planned and controlled.

Work Breakdown Structure Dictionary – The WBS dictionary documents the tasks, content, work and results for each work package, which are necessary to execute the WBS element. It includes often also deadlines, costs and technical performance.

Work Packages (WP) – It is the smallest, not further decomposed element in the work breakdown structure, which can be located on any project structure level. Each work package is provided with a work description, plan values, effort, duration, verifiable results (performance), resources and quality.

Work Remaining (WR) – Remaining work to the end of the project. The WR is equal to the budget at completion (BAC) minus Earned Value (EV).

Internet Links

The following internet links provides you access to the main EVM sources on the internet.

DoD Acquisition Community Connection, EVM-Homepage des DoD
https://acc.dau.mil/simplify/ev.php?ID=1500_201&ID2=DO_TOPIC

Office of the Under Secretary of Defense for Acquisition Technology, and Logistics: DoD EVM Implementation Guide (EVMIG), Guideline of "Defense for Acquisition, Technology, and Logistics"
http://www.acq.osd.mil/evm/

U.S. Department of Energy – Earned Value Management Information Center   http://energy.gov/management/office-management/operational-management/project-management/earned-value-management

NASA Earned Value Management   http://evm.nasa.gov/

PMI's College of Performance Management http://www.mycpm.org/

Earned Value Bibliography – comprehensive bibliography on EVM literature http://www.suu.edu/faculty/christensend/ev-bib.html

Australian Defense Organization – Industry Resources, Earned Value Management http://www.defence.gov.au/dmo/esd/evm/policy_docs.cfm

Niwot Ridge Resources – many useful EVM internet links
http://www.niwotridge.com/Resources/DomainLinks/EarnedValue.htm

All internet links in this book were current at time of printing of this book in 2014. However, it cannot be ruled out that some have changed in the meantime.

Appendix

Literature

Project Management Institute (2013), A Guide to the Project Management Body of Knowledge, Fifth Edition,

Project Management Institute (2011), Practice Standard for Earned Value Management, Second Edition

Walter H. Lipke (2012), Earned Schedule, lulu.com

Abba, W. (2000), How Earned Value Got to Primetime: A Short Look Back and Glance Ahead. Paper presented at the PMI Seminars & Symposium. Proceedings 20436.PDF, Houston, TX.

Abba Wayne (2007), Project Management using Earned Value Management, McGraw Hill

Quentin W. Fleming and Joel M. Koppelman, (2006) – Start with "simple" Earned Value on all your Projects– Crosstalk; The Journal of Defense Software Engineering

Quentin W. Flemming (2010), Earned Value Project Management, Project Management Inst; 4 edition

About the Author

Roland Wanner has been in the project business for 19 years already and has seen lots of projects – some of them successful, others that have failed. After his education as a mechanical engineer and industrial engineer he spent 5 years as a project manager and after that several years as a project controller and project portfolio manager in mechanical engineering and construction. For more than 10 years he's worked as a project management specialist, project portfolio manager and project office manager in the banking and insurance sector.

Your Opinion is Important to Us!

Thank you for purchasing this book! We have done our best to ensure high quality in content and design. Much effort was made to make this book as complete and correct as possible. However, it can't be ruled out that a mistake was made in one part of the book or another, whether contextual or grammatical. Maybe you think a certain piece of information is lacking or a certain subject should be expanded. We rely on your opinion!

We appreciate your ideas, thoughts and suggested corrections. Please send them to: info@pm-evm.com

Acknowledgments

With this first English Edition, I would like to thank the following for their unwavering support, trust and patience:

- My wonderful wife and my children, who gave me the moral support and time to write this book
- My translators and editors, especially Elisabeth Paregger and Elizabeth Stuart, who made this book as accurate as possible
- All the readers with their feedback and recommendations to make this and further books even better

Appendix

Index

A

Acceptance Criteria 52
actions, corrective 114
Actual Cost (AC) 72, 131
Actual Cost, incorrect time allocation 110
Actual Values 29
ACWP *see* Actual Cost (AC)
Air Force 20
American National Standards Institute 22
ANSI 22
ANSI/EIA-748 22, 33, 36, 71, 123, 131
APM Guideline 22
Apportioned Effort 131
AS4817-2006 22
Australian EVM-standard AS4817 33
Authorized Unpriced Work (AUW) 61, 62, 65, 131
Authorized Work 64, 131

B

BAC *see* Budget at Completion
Baseline 60, 131
Baseline Change Control 131
Baseline Freeze Date (BFD) 131
Baseline Review (BR) 132
Baseline Values 29
Baseline/Actual Comparison 26
Baseline/Target/Actual Comparison 28
BCWP *see* Earned Value
BCWS *see* Planned Value
Bottom-up estimate 100
Budget 132
Budget at Completion (BAC) 72, 132
Budgeted Cost of Work Performed (BCWP) 38
Budgeting in Earned Value Management 60
budgeting process 60

C

C/SCSC 20, *See* Cost/Schedule Control Systems Criteria
C/SSR *see* Cost/Schedule Status Report
CA *see* Control Account
CAM *see* Control Account Manager
CAP see, *see* Control Account Plan
CAP, appropriate size 59

CAP, example 58
CBB *see* Contract Budget Base
CFSR *see* Contract Funds Status Report
Change Control Process. 69
Clinger-Cohen Act 32
Contingency Reserve 66
Contract Budget Base (CBB) 61, 62, 132
contract changes 61, 63
Contract Data Requirements List (CDRL) 133
Contract Funds Status Report (CFSR) 133
Contract Target Cost (CTC) 133
Contract Target Price (CTP) 133
Contract Work Breakdown Structure (CWBS) 48, 133
Control Account 55, 64, 133
Control Account budget 64
Control Account Manager (CAM) 56, 58, 69, 133
Control Account Plan (CAP) 55, 69, 133
control measures 108
corporate failures 23
Corporate Governance Rules 23
corrective actions 93
Cost Account (CA) 133
cost exceeding 20
Cost Performance Index (CPI) **87**, 133
Cost Performance Report (CPR) 119, 133
cost target 60
Cost Variance (CV) **86**, 134
Cost/Schedule Control Systems Criteria 133
Cost/Schedule Control Systems Criteria" (C/SCSC) 20
Cost/Schedule Status Report (C/SSR) 134
CPI **87**, 132
CPI and SPI Grahic 89
CPI, significance 88
CPR *see* Cost Performance Report
C-specs 20
C-SSR Joint Guide 22
cumulative performance figures 89
CV **86**, *see* Cost Variance

D

Data and Variance Analysis 112
decision-making basis 114
defining measures 109
degree of completion 59
deliverables 59

142

deviations 112
Direct Costs 134
Discrete Effort 134
Distributed Budget 64
DoD 19, 60, 65, 70
DoD 35 criteria 20
DOE 60

E

EAC
- Optimistic Method 95
- Pessimistic Method 97
- Realistic Method 96
EAC(t) 134
early warning signals 93
early warning system 109
Earned Schedule 91, 134
Earned Value 36, 72, 134
Earned Value concept 20
Earned Value estimation methods 75
Earned Value Management Definitions 35
Earned Value Management Implementation Guide 22
Earned Value Management Systems 36
Earned Value Methods 75, 76
Earned Value, calculation 75
Estimate at Completion (EAC) 94, 134
Estimate to Complete (ETC) 100, 134
estimates 92
European Union 32
EV Method
- 0/100 79
- 50/50 78
- Apportioned Effort 84
- Percent Complete 80
- Percent Start/Percent Finish 78
- Units completed 83
- Weighted Milestones 81
- Weighted Milestones with Percent Complete 82
EV Method, how to choose one 85
EV Methods for Discrete Effort 77
evaluate project data 109
evaluation, fast 115
EVM
- 10 most important points 123
- collect data 108
- fundamental principles 34
- Graphs 117
- reputation 109
- simple on all projects 123
EVM and Risk Management 103

EVM evaluations, weekly 114
EVM Formulas 73
EVM Performance Figures, overview 73
EVM Standards and Guidelines 22
EVMIG 22
EVMS-criteria 123
EVM-System - Inputs und Outputs 111
EVM-Terms, old new 71

F

FASA, Title V 32
financial scandals 24
Fitzgerald's law 92
forecast, statistical 92, 100
forecasts 92

G

Government Performance and Results Act of 1993 32
GPRA 32

I

IBR *see* Integrated Baseline Review
Indirect Costs 135
Integrated Baseline Review (IBR) 135
Integrated Master Schedule (IMS) 135
Intent Guide 22
internal audit 23
interpreting EVM data 109

J

Joint Strike Fighter 121

K

key performance figures 34

L

Latest Revised Estimate (LRE) 135
legislations 23
Level of Effort (LOE) 53, 135
LOE *see* Level of Effort (LOE)
LRE *see* Latest Revised Estimate

M

make or buy 46
management accounting 12

Appendix

management control system 21
management culture 121
Management Reserve (MR) 63, 66, 135
managerial task 13
Master Project Schedule 135
milestone 82
milestone trend analysis 27
military projects 121

N

NASA 19
Negotiated Contract Cost (NCC) 61
network plan 20
new baseline 62

O

objective estimates 76
OMB (Office of Management and Budget) 32
Organizational Breakdown Structure (OBS) 56, 135
Over Target Baseline (OTB) 61, 62, 65, 136

P

Performance Measurement Baseline (PMS) 34, 49, 60, 63, 66, 136
PERT 20
PERT/cost and PERT/time 20
physical completed 30
physical progress 38, 75
Plan/EAC/ACTUAL comparison 16
Planned Value (PV) 136
Planning Package 64, 136
Planning Process 43
PMB 65, *see* Performance Measurement Baseline
PMBOK 13, 22, 43, 50, 71
problem indicators 115
profit/fee 61, 62
progress milestone 81
project control process 15
Project Control vs. Controlling 12
project control, internal vs. external 16
project end date 92
project execution control cycle 17
project financial analyst 13
project management software 120
project management system 20

project monitoring, potential problem indicators 115
project planning
 cost-benefit ratio 51
Project planning 42
project scope 60
project scope planning 45
project status meetings, weekly 114
project structuring 47

R

recovery budget 62
Relation between EVM-Performance Figures 101
Replanning 114, 136
Reporting 105
reporting cycle 80, 121
reporting cycles, shorter 54, 120
reporting dates 59
reporting degree completion 54
reporting period 77, 113
reporting work 53
Reporting, added value 106
Reporting, poor quality 106
Reporting, project size 119
Reporting, U.S. Government 119
Reprogramming 62, 136
Request or Requirement **32**
requirement specification 45, 48
Reserves and Buffers 66
Residual Values 29, 30
Responsibility Assignment Matrix (RAM) 136
Risk Management 103
risks 66

S

Sarbanes-Oxley Act 23, 32
Schedule Performance Index (SPI) 88, 137
Schedule Reserve 68
Schedule Variance (SV) 86, 137
scope of work 48, 57
slack 68
SOX 23
SPI 88
SPI and CPI behavior 91
SPI(t) 137
Statement of Work 58
Status Report 114
subcontractor 32
subjective evaluation 77

sub-project 46, 50
Summary Level Planning Package (SLPP) 63
sunk cost argument 92
Supervisor's Estimate 80
support activity 84
SV converges to 0 90
SV(t) 137

T

TAB see Total Allocated Budget (TAB)
Target cost 28
Target Values 29
TCPI see To Complete Performance Index
Technical Performance Measurement (TPM) 137
time buffer 68
To Complete Performance Index (TCPI) 99, 137
To Complete Schedule Performance Index TSPI(t) 137
Total Allocated Budget (TAB) 61, 62, 137
Traditional cost analysis 26
transparency 25
trust, analysis is better 115
truth 24

U

U.S. Department of Defense 32
UB Siehe Undistributed Budget (UB)
Undefinitized Change Order 65
Undistributed Budget (UB) 63, 137

V

VAC see Variance at Completion
Value Management System Criteria 21
Variance at Completion (VAC) 98, 138

W

WBS see Work Breakdown Structure and Earned Value Management 49
WBS element 59
WBS level 59
WBS-Dictionary 138
work
- classification of work 52
- apportioned effort 52
- discrete effort 52
- Level of Effort (LOE) 53
work authorization 69
Work Authorization Document (WAD) 70, 138
work breakdown structure 47
- basic concept 48
Work Breakdown Structure 45
Work Breakdown Structure (WBS) 56, 138
work package 50
  8/80 rule 51
  reporting rule 51
Work Package 138
Work Package (WP) 64
Work Package Acceptance 52
work package manager 59
work package problems 112
work package size 53, 113
work package size and duration 51
Work Packages and Earned Value Management 53
work packages, only a few 110
work packages, too big 108
work progress, determine easier 109
Work Remaining (WR) 138
Worst-case scenario 97

Appendix

Appendix

Appendix

Printed in Great Britain
by Amazon